MESSIAH IN ME AND I IN HIM

*...the glorious riches **of this mystery**, which
is Messiah in you, **the hope of glory**! Col.1:27*

Kay Bascom

Olive Press
צהר 🔥 זית

In

A New Testament based study
of how the Messiah
continues to be
incarnated in His people

Kay Bascom

On MESSIAH IN ME AND I IN HIM

ISBN 978-1-941173-30-5

Copyright © 2017 by Kay Bascom

A *Messiah Mystery* Resources publication

Published in the USA

Published by

Olive Press Messianic and Christian Publisher
www.olivepresspublisher.org
olivepressbooks@gmail.com

Cover background images from Bing.com/images

Our prayer at Olive Press is that we may help make the Word of Adonai fully known, that it spread rapidly and be glorified everywhere. We hope our books help open people's eyes so they will turn from darkness to Light and from the power of the adversary to God and to trust in ישוע Yeshua (Jesus). (From II Thess. 3:1; Col. 1:25; Acts 26:18,15 NRSV *New Revised Standard Version* and CJB, the Complete Jewish Bible.)

The author's website: www.messiahmysteryresources.org

My prayer is not for them alone. I pray also for those who will believe in me through their message, that all of them may be one, Father, just as you are <u>in</u> me and I am <u>in</u> you. May they also be <u>in</u> us so that the world may believe that you have sent me...I have made you known to them, and will continue to make you known in order that the love you have for me may be <u>in</u> them and that I myself may be <u>in</u> them.

John 17:20-21, 26

TABLE OF CONTENTS

INTRODUCTION

Welcome to 𝓘𝓝 studies that focus on the Messiah's continuing incarnation in the New Covenant people. 𝓘𝓝 discloses seven aspects of the Holy Spirit's relationship to the believer. These marvelous provisions are the basis of every believer's enablement. We need the Spirit's illumination to believe these truths and cooperate with their dynamic in our daily lives. We need spiritual enlightenment (Ephesians 1:18), for as the Chinese brother Watchman Nee affirmed in his book *The Normal Christian Life* (page 101), "The revelation of the fact of the Spirit's indwelling can revolutionize the life of any Christian!"

Why 𝓘𝓝**?** The most important relational word in the New Testament may well be "in." Over and over, the Spirit of God explains that all that comes to the believer is due to being in Christ. This study explores that wealth. Paul expresses the unfolding of the mystery of the Messiah in this way:

> *To them God has chosen to make known among the Gentiles the glorious riches of this mystery, which is Christ in you, the hope of glory. ...My purpose is that they may be encouraged in heart and united in love, so that they may have the full riches of complete understanding, in order that they may know the mystery of God, namely, Christ, in whom are hidden all the treasures of wisdom and knowledge.*
> ~ Colossians 1:27; 2:2-3

𝓘𝓝 **is a companion to a previous study called** 𝓐𝓛𝓛 that traces the presence of the Messiah throughout the Old Testament. The Scriptures testified to the Messiah, as *Yeshua* (as He was called during the Incarnation) made clear in Luke 24:25-27. 𝓐𝓛𝓛 focuses on seven roles of the Coming One as they emerged in the Old Covenant period and then unfolded more fully at the time of the Messianic Son's Incarnation. While the Incarnation may seem to have been concluded at the time of the Messiah's Ascension, the New Testament unfolds a new marvel. The Spirit of God continues the Incarnation ("embodiment") thereafter, in the believers. When we are included in Him, all that is His becomes ours. Knowing this and being enabled by

His indwelling Spirit, His people come alive to continue His Incarnation in the world, "until He comes." Let us live fully by the marvelous resources that are ours IN CHRIST!

ALL and *All* survey the Bible with the Messiah as their moving "marker." These panoramic overviews are meant to provide a road map through the Scriptures. They may seem overloaded with references, compared to studies designed for discussion, yet understanding God's broad truth can enrich other types of study.

Here is a thumbnail sketch of the course's orientation:

Source – The Bible (II Timothy 3:16-17; I Peter 1:10-12)

Focus – *Yeshua*/ Jesus (Hebrews 12:2)

Dynamic – The Holy Spirit (Ephesians 3:16-17a)

Viewpoint – Panoramic and progressive (Ephesians 2:3-10)

Method – Shadow and Substance
(Colossians 2:17, Hebrews 8:5; 9:24; 10:1)

Calling – To present the mystery (Colossians 1:26-29)

Prayer – To be filled with the fullness of God (Ephesians 3:14-21)

Setting the scene: *Carefully consider* four orientation clues opening each chapter: 1. "Aspect" of being "IN Christ." 2. Study's subject. 3. Key question. 4. Biblical sources (Old Testament basis, and progressing through the New Testament).

♥ **A heart symbol** appears at the close of each study. That section calls for a response from the heart. Webster defines the heart as "one's innermost character, feelings, or inclinations." J.I. Packer calls the heart "the motivational and dynamic core of our being." That is where we meet God.

An explanation: The author regrets the text's distracting inconsistency when it comes to capitalization of pronouns referring to deity. Unfortunately the NIV version most used in this document (like many versions) does not capitalize them. If the text uses caps (so basic to the author's thinking) and the Bible does not, a variation occurs every time Scripture is quoted. Quotations from other writers' works involve this mixture of treatment, as well; yet they must be quoted as originally written. Apologies!

Your adventure: A Bible study can be a personal investigation, or a group experience. Some groups prefer to spend two sessions on each chapter. How many references are investigated, how earnest the accompanying prayer, how serious the appropriation—these aspects will vary. Let us remember that *it is the Holy Spirit on whom we must depend for life-giving results* in the whole process. May your understanding be deepened, your joy increased, and your endurance strengthened as you depend upon the Spirit of God to take you on this adventure!

Kay Bascom

Study 1

"In"

Why is the little word "in" so vital?

Introduction: When we get down to it, religion can be dry and impractical. Remember the distinction, "Christianity is not a religion, it is a relationship." Life is built on relationships. How can we experience our faith in a relationship sense? That is what being "in" is about — something of deep significance that enriches and energizes the believer's life.

Context: *In*'s overarching theme is expressed in *Yeshua's* prayer in John 17, just before He went to Gethsemane and on to the Cross. (Using "*Yeshua*" helps us to think of Him in His 1st century, Hebrew cultural context.) He is praying at the end of a long evening of fellowship at the Passover meal with His disciples. John's chapters 13-17 are sometimes called the "Holy of Holies" of Scripture. They report that last night before the cross. God's Spirit has recorded for His people this intimate rendezvous in which *Yeshua* opened His heart to His band of disciples, and to His Father. What was His uppermost concern? How did He pray? Amazingly, we are included in that prayer!

What final instructions would you expect the leader of a religious movement to give at his departure? Would he outline the next steps they were to implement? Would he state some official transfer of authority? Humanly speaking, we can imagine what some necessities might be to insure continuation of the movement that would come to be called "Christianity." But the Messiah was not "humanly speaking," He was divinely speaking. Instead of an outline of a program, or the instatement of a successor, He talked with them about what He knew to be of highest priority. If possible, read chapters 13-17 of John at one sitting, as a whole. Absorb them by the help of the Holy Spirit. If they were crucial then, they are crucial now.

About what did our Lord talk with His Father at the end of this night of consultation with His disciples? *Yeshua*'s prayer in John 17 is striking in focus, and its depths are unfathomable. Such spiritual mysteries as the relationship between God and His Son cannot be reduced to human grasp. They can only be spiritually sensed by the work of the Holy Spirit within the reader. Our starting place is to ask the Spirit of God to reveal what He wants to show us. He must enlighten us, or we remain spiritually deaf and blind.

Overhearing Jesus' prayer in John 17, consider what He said to His Father:

From John 17:1-5:

Q. What did He mean by, "The time has come"? He often said it had not come, as in John 7:6. He said it was "near" in Matthew 26:18.

Q. By *what* would the Father and Son "glorify" each other?

Q. What was *Yeshua*'s definition of "eternal life"?

Q. What glimpse does He give of "before the world began"?

Q. What does *Yeshua*'s prayer reveal about His identity?

From John 17:6-11:

Q. What two things did *Yeshua* say He had done?

Q. What two things had His disciples done?

From John 17:12-19:
Q. What things did He ask the Father to do for His disciples?

Q. What is the source behind the word "sent" — found in verse 8, 18, 21, 23, 25?

From John 17:20-26:
Q. Who does *Yeshua* pray for at the end?

Q. What does He ask for them — actually, also for us?

Q. By what relationship does He expect to prove who sent Him to the world? (verses 21, 23, 25)

Q. What marvelous assurances to you as a believer do you find in verses 24 and 25?

This intimate prayer — a consultation between Father and Son — has been a great gift to His people down through the ages. What was heaviest on the Lord's heart as He had to take leave of these men and women with whom He had intimately spent three years?

For clues, look over our Lord's Prayer in John 17:12-26 and notice what eight or so words are repeated over and over (not counting the word "in"). *Write the key words below and ask the Spirit of God to give you eyes to glimpse the mystery of how our Lord meant them to be related:*

Verse reference:	Key words:

Try to draw a diagram of the relationships "pictured" in John 17:12-26 — the "in" relationships — (between who and who).

What does it mean that He uses this word "in" so many times? "In" is a tiny preposition. A preposition in grammar is a "relationship" word. To be "in" is the opposite of "out" and different than being "by" or "with." It is not "above" or "below" — it is "in." Grasp that meaning and that experience, and you have the essence of what *Yeshua* reveals to be the core of His relationship with His people — not His doctrine or rules, but His relationship.

"In-ness" tries to express a mysterious relationship. One analogy might be the relationship between a human father and son. The son has been "in" the father (his loins), and the father is "in" the son (his heredity). A son's genes and often his thinking reflect the father. For another analogy in Scripture, take Adam and Eve's being created "in the image of God" (Genesis1:27). His "image" included them both. Humans needed to be sexual to reproduce. God is spirit. He is not sexual, nor temporal, but eternal.

Earlier in the evening, before His prayer, *Yeshua* tried to prepare them for the new relationship the Godhead was about to launch. *Look at what He revealed about "in" in these passages and write down a phrase for "remembering" these key teachings:*

John 14:20

John 15:1-4

John 15:5-7

John 15:9-17

Being "in Christ" is so crucial that the New Testament continues to portray this relationship.

➢   John 13-17 prepares and prays for it.

➢   Acts shows how it began to happen.

➢   The Letters explain its depths.

➢   Revelation reveals the outcome of being "in Christ" or not.

Therefore, our *IN* study will move through the New Testament in that order.

However, it is not as if the idea of "in" takes off on its own. It is based on the "all" of the Old Testament — all the Scriptures that *Yeshua* revealed about Himself! (See Luke 24:25-27.) This is a mystery that only the Spirit of God can make real to us. Before going on to see how that happened, and how it was experienced by the early church, we need to go back and summarize what the ALL was that was being transferred to being IN the believers after Pentecost. Therefore Study 2 is called "Integration." It integrates the Old Testament "all" that *Yeshua* stated on the Emmaus Road with the New Testament "in" that we are about to explore in the rest of these studies.

♥ A heart symbol at the close of each study suggests a focus meant to encourage us to make real heart engagement with God's truth, so that it can transform us at the core of our lives.

♥ *Do I really want the Word of God to change my heart and life in a dynamic way?*

Prayer *is our place to begin any attempt to understand and experience God's revelation. Paul's prayer to the Father is a basic one for us to claim:*

I pray that out of his glorious riches he may strengthen you with power through his Spirit in your inner being, so that Christ may dwell in your hearts through faith. And I pray that you, being rooted and established in love, may have power together with all the saints, to grasp how wide and long and high and deep is the love of Christ, and to know this love that surpasses knowledge – that you may be filled to the measure of all the fullness of God.

~ Ephesians 3:16-19

Ω

Study 2

INTEGRATION

What ties the Old and New Testament together? What is the Bible all about?

(Drawn from both Old and New Testaments — and especially Matthew)

Introduction: Literate people have the opportunity to investigate the world's most famous book. Great books deserve to be read as a whole. The serious reader who wants to know what a book is about asks questions like, "Who is the author, what is the theme, who are the characters, what is the problem being explored?"

Context: Books employ certain elements. What historical catastrophe is the Biblical record portraying and trying to resolve? This panoramic story has many characters, but who is the one around whom the plot turns? How does the Bible itself answer that question? We can find summary passages in the Bible that give us these keys. We can see how the story develops and who turns out to be the real hero. We can notice how the hero's significance is unfolded along the plot line, often by foreshadowing, or with clues that will later lead to his identification. When the main problem is encountered near the climax of the book, the plot takes a certain shape, and we realize what the story has really been about.

Authorship is one of the intriguing aspects of the Bible. Scripture is authored by many people over a period of many centuries. That would seem to yield a hodge-podge of stories and details that would not add up to a consistent plot like one conceived by one author. Yet the Bible's story is a united whole.

Who wrote the Bible? Those who have deeply studied the Bible have found an answer to this authorship question. We call it "the inspiration of the Scriptures." (See II Timothy 3:16.) The 66 books are tied together with such intricateness, such unity, that a guiding hand had to orchestrate them. The text itself declares that the Spirit of God did this. Human writers interacted with God and expressed His truth through their particular thought patterns and writing styles.

"Are the New Testament Documents Reliable?" That is the title of a valuable book by Biblical scholar F.F. Bruce. His strong "yes," after careful research, deals with a basic prerequisite upon which the Bible student counts. Since the lst Century, many a "Jesus" has been constructed out of false theology or man's imagination. Only the Scriptures can be trusted to show us the true Jesus in His own context, and guided by the Teacher and Counselor who Jesus appointed to that task. (See John 16:13-15.)

Unfortunately, the Bible has been published in two parts — "Old" and "New" Testaments. Throughout both, it is the early foreshadowing and later revelation — the early predictions and later fulfillments — that indicate the *inseparableness* of the two covenants' disclosures. The plot's progression and resolution should not be separated. They must be kept whole. This unity can be investigated in a number of ways.

Three demonstrations of the Bible's unity can be researched by examining it in terms of: 1. Foreshadowing 2. Prophetic consistency 3. Summaries.

First, "foreshadowing": *IN*'s companion study, *ALL*, approached the Bible from the "shadow and substance" standpoint, a term used, for instance, in Hebrews 8:5; 10:1 and Colossians 2:17. *ALL* traced seven roles of the coming "Anointed One." The Messiah was long awaited by the Covenant People. We can find these foreshadowed roles re-appearing in the first book of the New Testament. Realize that Matthew was written some 400 years after the Old Testament closed.

Notice Matthew's allusions to Jesus' fulfillments of Old Testament roles:

The seed of woman: Matthew 1:18

(Background: Genesis 3:15)

The son of Abraham: Matthew 1:1, 17

(Background: Genesis 22:18)

The sacrificial Lamb: Matthew 20:18-19; 20:28

(Background: Genesis 22:8)

The ultimate Priest: Matthew 21:12-13

(See Hebrews 3:1; 5:14-16; 7:11-17)

The Prophet to come: Matthew 21:11

(Background: Deut. 18:15-19)

The Davidic King – Matthew 1:1; 12:23

(Background: II Samuel 7:12-16)

The Host of the Feasts – Matthew 12:8, Matthew 26:26-29

(Background Leviticus 23:3-5)

Second, prophetic consistency: Notice that the two Testaments share principal characters and their related prophecies. The first book of the New Testament is full of quotations and references to statements in the Old. Other New Testament books are similar. *For example, here are references to specific prophets woven throughout the book of Matthew:*

David: Matthew 1:1, 20-21; 22:42-45

Isaiah: Matthew 1:23; 4:14; 8:17; 12:17; 13:14; 15:7

Jeremiah: Matthew 2:18; 27:9

Daniel: Matthew 24:15

Zechariah: Matthew 21:4

Frequently the prophets are quoted, assuming that Jewish readers would know the Old Testament sources. *A few examples:*

Matthew 1:23, quoting Isaiah 7:14

Matthew 2:5-6, quoting Micah 5:2

Matthew 4:4, quoting Deuteronomy 8:3

Matthew 9:13, quoting Hosea 6:6

Matthew 10:35, quoting Micah 7:6

Matthew 11:10, quoting Malachi 3:1

Matthew 27:46, quoting David's Psalm 22

We can learn much by noticing how the classics are written. They are not in outline form. The plot is woven throughout, and must be read carefully. The reader pulls together what already is known of the characters. At the end of the story, the importance of small details and key conversations emerge. The message all comes into focus! This is why the Bible needs to be understood as a whole, right through to the end, from Genesis to Revelation. Even though the 66 books have been put down by various writers in different centuries, the Author has known the whole story from the beginning. His story is non-fiction.

Third, summaries that appear in book after book: Summary statements about the burden of the Biblical message are found right within it. Many voices testify to who is the central character of God's message, and what is claimed for Him. Here are a few "summary passages" stretching from Matthew to Revelation. *Who is the focus? What is claimed for Him? What historical continuity is mentioned? What purpose is stated?"*

Matthew 5:17-18 (*Yeshua* speaking)

Mark 1:1-8

Luke 24:25-27 (the risen *Yeshua* speaking)

John 1:1-18; 20:29-31

Acts 2:22-36

Romans 16:25-27

Ephesians 1:3-14

Philippians 2:6-11

Colossians 1:15-20

Hebrews 1:1-4

Revelation 22:13, 16 (the glorified Christ speaking)

From the summary passages above, we see how the threads of the Bible weave back and forth between the two Testaments in fascinating ways! The pattern of God's eternal purpose emerges when looked at as a whole. Cross references in the margins of study Bibles lead the searcher around through the Bible in ways that can open up whole new vistas of relationships and meaning.

From this firm Old Testament base, the rest of the *JM* studies launch into the New Testament. The New Covenant is not to be separated from the Old. The New does not supersede the Old, but shows how God's purposes are being progressively completed. The New Testament's testimony to the Incarnation, the Resurrection, and the Ascension of the Messiah completes the ancient story. Our God does not change. However, the historical dynamic changed in the lst Century AD on the day of Pentecost. By the work of the Holy Spirit, the offer of redemption fanned out from the Hebrew people to the whole world.

The New Testament Letters reflect this wide inclusiveness. The bad news in Genesis is universal sin. The intermediate news is the preparation of a Redeemer to come out of the Chosen People. The good news is the arrival of the Messiah and His offer of redemption to all, to anybody, to everybody! John 3:16-17 records the famous "whosoever will" invitation.

Jesus/*Yeshua* is totally inclusive. We, however, may exclude ourselves. This is the unavoidable choice each of us has to make.

♥ *What choice am I making?*

PRAYER:

Oh Lord, work in me to warm my heart to your truth. Give me a hunger to see You and Your marvelous plan in a fuller way! Surely this prayer would be consistent to ask, as *Yeshua* encouraged us to pray – "in His name."

Ω

Hold on to the INTEGRATION KEY to Scripture:

In the past God spoke to our forefathers through the prophets at many times and in various ways, but in these last days he has spoken to us by his Son, whom he appointed heir of all things, and through whom he made the universe. The Son is the radiance of God's glory and the exact representation of his being, sustaining all things by his powerful word.

Hebrews 1:1-3a

Study 3

INCARNATION

Why is the choice between belief and unbelief so crucial?

(Drawn largely from the Gospels)

Introduction: Suppose Jesus had never come to earth. How would the world be different? How would your life be different? Who would have won the victory? Who would know the difference?

For another perspective, suppose we had only the Old Testament. Twenty centuries later, who would be holding on to the promise of a Messiah, let alone a "fore-runner" to the Messiah prophesied in Malachi? Not the wider world, surely. With no Christianity in the world to remind them, would the larger Jewish population even be expecting a Messiah anymore?

The Incarnation was like a window, open briefly, through which humans could safely see God. Consider, why do unbelieving Jews and believing Christians today generally see God so differently? The key: Believers can see God through the window of Jesus the Christ. Many unbelievers have not been allowed to or not chosen to look through that window. Believers long to share their understanding of God as seen "in the face of Jesus Christ." (II Corinthians 4:6 KJV)

Context: "The Elijah" link

Imagine 400 years of silence before the Incarnation, with no prophets speaking. Faintly remembering an Old Testament promise of "Elijah's return" before the Messiah would come, only very earnest believers would have held on to that hope in Israel. Trodden under by the Romans, Jerusalem still received yearly pilgrims to the feasts, but the ecclesiastical leadership was divided and rife with hypocrisy. In the councils of God, when "the time had fully come" (Galatians 4:4), the Father sent the Son into the world. The moment for the Incarnation had arrived! "The Word became flesh" (John 1:14) and thereafter, we have been given the assurance from Jesus that, "He who has seen me has seen the Father" (John 14:9).

Had the Israelites received no prior notice? Yes, they had, and that is where the New Testament begins. All four of the Gospels document the appearance of the Messiah's "forerunner" (told in Matthew 3:1-17, Mark 1:2-4, Luke 1:5-25, and John 1:19-23). This was what Israel had been waiting for ever since the Old Testament went silent with the last prophet's "Elijah promise" (Malachi 4:5) given some 400 years before.

John the Baptizer's story in Matthew, Mark, and John records the Forerunner's encounters with *Yeshua* when the two men were in their adulthood. However, Luke (probably informed by Mary) gives us the priceless record of Gabriel's announcement of the miraculous birth of the baby to be named "John" to Elizabeth and Zechariah.

From Luke 1:5-25, consider these questions:

➢ What dating, names, and ancestries are documented?

➢ Had you been Zechariah, what do you think you'd have felt?

➢ Exactly what did the angel say, and who was he quoting? (verse 17)

➢ What are the miraculous aspects we can surmise from the passage?

Tracing "the Elijah:" The rest of Luke 1 and chapter 2 tell us about Gabriel's announcement to Mary, her response, her visit to Elizabeth, the birth of "John," and finally the birth of Jesus. To John's father, Gabriel said that John would "go on before the Lord in the spirit and power of Elijah" (Luke 1:13-17). Of course Zechariah would recognize the angel's quotation in Luke 1:17 from Malachi 4:5-6.

The Forerunner's role: When *Yeshua* began His public ministry, John had prepared His way, preaching a baptism of repentance, and then directing his followers to the One who was to come.

From John 1:19-29:

What did John the Baptist understand about who he himself was? (John 1:23 quotes Isaiah 40:3)

When questioned, John did not say that he was "Elijah." Why do you think that was left to Jesus to say, and why at the time Jesus said it? (See the accounts in Luke 7:26-28 and Matthew 11:7-14.)

The Old Covenant gave preparation for John's announcement: John pointed his spiritual community to the person of Jesus, calling him "the Lamb of God" (John 1:29). This name was based upon the Jewish community's preparation for centuries, focused upon God's provision of a lamb as a substitutional sacrifice in place of a human's death penalty for sin. From Eden forward, this practice was imbedded in God's provision for restoring sinful people to fellowship with the Holy One. The lamb's role was heightened the night of the Exodus from Egypt, was repeated for centuries in Tabernacle and Temple worship, and was referred to in prophecy, such as Isaiah's 53rd chapter.

The long-awaited appearance of these two, the Forerunner and the Messiah, happened only once in history. People kept asking both of them, "Are you the Elijah? Are you the Christ?" Jesus identified John, and He identified Himself over and over again, had they really been hearing. The New Testament gives us the record of His telling them, and of their blindness. We are in danger of the same unbelief — the one sin Jesus said was deadliest.

Human incredulity: The event of the Incarnation had no predecessor. It was a totally new experience for the human race. He looked like an ordinary man walking their paths in sandals like their own. *Yeshua* puzzled them. He kept saying and doing amazing things, so people kept asking, "How could this be?" He kept demonstrating His identity, but they failed to "put two and two together." They asked one question after another. We would have had similar questions.

> "Who gave you this authority?" (in Matthew 21:23-27)
> "Who can forgive sins but God alone? (in Mark 2:7-12)
> "Who is this? Even wind and waves obey him." (in Mark 4:41)

When the leaders asked who he was, they shut their ears to His answer. Over and over He prefaced His answer with the "I AM" designation that God gave Moses for Himself at the burning bush (Exodus 3:14). Jesus added one identifier or description of Himself after another: "I AM the Light of the World, the Bread of Life (do you hear echoes of the Tabernacle?), the Door, the Good Shepherd, the Way, the Truth, the Life!" And "before Abraham was born, I am." That last claim (reported in the furious encounter in John 8:58) angered the authorities more than any. John 10:33 tells us they charged Him with blasphemy: "because you, a mere man, claim to be God." On the surface and without the illumination of the Spirit of God, we can sympathize with this conclusion. That is exactly what *Yeshua* was claiming.

What the Jewish leadership didn't ask Jesus, was, "WHY have you come?" (We might be as blind as 1st Century people, not asking, "What is God saying to us, to me?") The Messiah told them anyway.

What reason did Jesus give for His first appearance on earth, in these passages?

Luke 5:32

John 12:27-28

John 12:47

Matthew 20:28

The leadership seemed to have no sense of need, much as we often fail to realize ours. The Trinity was dealing with issues of cosmic proportion. Their purpose was to undo the Fall, to triumph over Satan, to give the human race a new Head, to bring us back into fellowship, and to overcome darkness with the Light.

Having given the generation of His Incarnation every opportunity to accept Him, *Yeshua* knew what was in the heart of man. He knew He would be rejected, and told them this repeatedly, before it happened. *Consider these examples, two veiled in parables and four clearly stated:*

Matthew 21:33-44 (the tenants who killed the owner's son)

Luke 16:19-31 (the rich man, Lazarus, and the resurrection)

Matthew 20:17-19

Luke 9:21-22

Luke 18:31-33

John 12:23-36.

We today have less reason to disbelieve. By now we know the end of the story. We have the added facts of the Resurrection, the Messiah's Ascension and Enthronement, the gift of the Holy Spirit to believers, and the testimony of the New Testament. We've been given a perspective from Eternity — especially in the book of John.

The gospel of John, in contrast to the synoptic gospels (Matthew Mark and Luke) begins Jesus' story where Genesis began, "in the beginning." We are working on a wider canvas now, stretching out into eternity. John calls Jesus "the Word." At creation, God spoke a word, and it *was*. During Jesus' Incarnation, God spoke through His Son, as asserted by Hebrews 1:1-3.

Look carefully at the revelations in John 1:1-18:

Who is the Word, and who and where was He "in the beginning"?

What claims are made for Him in verse 3 and 10-11?

John the Baptizer appears in verses 6-8 and 15. What is his role?

What does Jesus give those who receive Him? (12-13)

How are Moses and Jesus compared in verse 17?

What do verses 14 and 18 add to verse 1 about "the Word"?

"He did it with a word," as E. Stanley Jones put it, looking at the Bible's amazing statement about the Son of God "sustaining all things by his powerful word" (in Hebrews 1:3). That cosmos-encompassing claim was exemplified even by Jesus' interactions on earth.

> He sustained the world of health around Him — cured the sick with a word. He cleansed and sustained the inner life of men by casting out devils and did it with a word. He lifted the inner guilt from a diseased soul and body and did it with a word. "Thy sins are forgiven thee." He stilled the tempest of raging sea, and He did it with a word. He raised the dead: "Lazarus come forth"; "My daughter arise" — and he did it with a word....He opened the gates of Paradise to a dying thief and did it with a word: "Today thou shalt be with me in Paradise."... He did it in the little; now through the little they saw Him doing it in the big — in the microcosm and in the macrocosm. They had to see it in the little before they could see it in the big. The Word had to become flesh before it could become cosmos. (E. Stanley Jones, *The Word Became Flesh,* page 360.)

Here are three kinds of evidence on which to base our response:

1. *Cosmic identity:* We have <u>testimonies</u> from His Father, His disciples, and Himself woven throughout the four biographies of the New Testament. We have seen how winsome the Savior's character was, as people of all walks of life responded to him—the crowds, His disciples, the poor, the sick, the desperate, women, children, and above all, "sinners." Jesus said, *"He who has seen me has seen the Father"* (John 14:9).

2. *Cosmic power:* We have seen His authentication inherent in the <u>works and miracles</u> He manifested. Who but God could heal the sick, feed the thousands, calm the storm, drive out demons, forgive sins, and even raise the dead? *Yeshua* said, *"...at least believe on the evidence of the miracles themselves"* (John 14:11b).

3. *Cosmic battle:* Satan's attack on the human race issued in a battle fought over the centuries. He attacked Jesus as well, and

tried to block His redeeming purpose. *Yeshua* stayed faithful and accomplished <u>the work of redemption</u> as the Lamb of God. Only after the Resurrection was God's rescue plan further revealed by the Spirit of God, so that we can glimpse the whole picture. Paul wrote, *"For he has rescued us from the dominion of darkness and brought us into the kingdom of the Son he loves, in whom we have redemption, the forgiveness of sins"* (Colossians 1:13-14).

The Identity crisis—their destiny and ours: It is really the Messiah's questions that men and women need to answer. Jesus repeatedly asked His followers, *"Who do you say that I am?"* Their destiny hung and our destiny hangs on the answer each of us gives.

♥ *What do I choose to believe about Jesus' identity?*

They asked, "After your departure, how are we to be sustained?" His disciples were finally believing, but they asked that question and don't we too? Knowing that after the crucifixion, He would be glorified, He prepared His disciples the night before the Cross. He promised them that they would see Him again, that they would eventually be with Him, and that He would return to earth a second time in glory. Meanwhile, He was sending them the Comforter in His place in the interim. He assured them that the Spirit of God would continue to reveal Himself to them (John 15:26; 16:13-14). A whole new dynamic was about to come into action, one that would soon be inaugurated. With that event, the book of Acts begins.

This Inauguration of the age of the Holy Spirit is the subject of our fourth study. This new dynamic is the one in which we presently live. Therefore, it is imperative that we understand and cooperate with the amazing resources that God's indwelling Spirit provides for us.

Prayer:

Dear Father, awaken me to the wonders and implications of Jesus' Incarnation and the Spirit's inauguration into my own life!

Ω

Hold on to the INCARNATION KEY to the Spirit's dynamic!

In the beginning was the Word, and the Word was with God, and the Word was God. He was with God in the beginning ...The Word became flesh, and made his dwelling among us. We have seen his glory, the glory of the One and Only, who came from the Father, full of grace and truth.

John 1:1-2, 14

Study 4

INAUGURATION
How did Pentecost change the world?

(Drawn principally from the book of Acts)

Introduction: What does "inauguration" mean? Webster says that to inaugurate is to bring about the beginning, to dedicate ceremoniously, or to observe the beginning formally — as in the inauguration of a new president. How does "inauguration" apply to God's kingdom? The arrival of the Spirit brought about this unique beginning. The events of the Day of Pentecost demonstrated that the risen Son's Exaltation ceremony had happened in Heaven. "Exalted to the right hand of God, he has received from the Father the promised Holy Spirit and has poured out what you now see and hear" (Acts 2:33). Look back at John 7:37-39 for further explanation.

Context: God's commitment to Adam's race has remained the same since the Fall — to make redemption available to the entire world! The Old Testament shows us how He chose to set up His rescue from a tiny launching pad, Abraham's family, eventually called "Israel." Then the New Testament shows us how God enveloped the whole world (called "the nations" or "Gentiles") in His plan for humanity's redemption. The Incarnation is the point of intersection between the two — the time when the Deliverer *Yeshua* announced that "the Kingdom of God is at hand."

***Yeshua* used an analogy to explain how radical this change-over would be.** How did His analogy of putting "new wine into old wineskins" clarify this unique period when the King was inaugurating His kingdom? *Look at Jesus' clues in Matthew 9:14-17, and give thought to what you think He might have included in "old" and what in "new."*

Yeshua used a parable about a landowner to describe what was happening. The owner went to a far country, leaving his servant as his agent. *How does the story in Mark 12:1-12 (quoting Psalm 118:22-23) predict how Israel would respond to the Son God sent?*

Who are "the others" to whom the owner would give the vineyard?

How did Jesus explain heaven's mysteries to earth-bound, time-limited sons and daughters of Adam? As He neared the climax of His Incarnation, Jesus gave parable-framed glimpses of the mysterious process that would reach from the Son's first coming to His second. His Kingdom parables are not isolated little stories. On the contrary, each weaves a different strand into the tapestry that Jesus was unveiling when He gave clue after clue, saying, "the Kingdom of heaven is like...a landowner who hired...like a landowner that planted....like a king who prepared a wedding banquet...like ten virgins who...like a man who gave talents to..." (See Matthew 21-25 for these parables.) Ponder these strands to get a feel for the heart of the owner-King and His royal Son, and the condition of humanity — faulty or faithful — over the centuries.

♥ *What warnings and encouragements do these parables give each of us for our own season of waiting and testing?*

JH **'s movement:** Our study is moving now from the Gospels to Acts — from the Incarnation to the Inauguration — but our Lord has already told us what to expect as history draws near to "the end of the story." At the end, judgment time does arrive. Just before the week of His passion, Jesus' parables gave way to blunt statements of what will eventually happen. "When the Son of Man comes in his glory...he will sit on his throne in heavenly glory. All the nations will be gathered before him..." (Matthew 25:31-32).

But back to the 1st Century and Acts: God's timing is exact. Consider the significance of the timing of each fulfillment between the Passion of Christ and Pentecost. Understanding God's use of the Feasts of Israel helps us appreciate the significance of the Messiah's consecutive fulfillment of the first four feasts: Passover, Unleavened Bread, First Fruits; and 50 days later, Pentecost. (*JH*'s companion study, *ALL*, explored these feasts.) Imagine yourself to be among Jesus' disciples right after that intense Passion Week chronicled by the Gospels, but before God's next step, recorded in Acts.

♥ *What would you have been expecting?*

The Biblical message was proceeding step by step. The Gospels tell us what happened when Jesus' parable's "owner's son" came back to earth, knowing He would need to die for the salvation of the world. The book of Acts records what happened when the King inaugurated a whole new Age to draw the world to the King who gave His life for them. Acts 2 gives us an historical account of this new creation, and the New Testament Letters were written between its members. For example, look at how most of the letters begin, as in Romans 1:7, I Corinthians 1:2, Galatians 1:1, Ephesians 1:1, etc. *What is this new entity?*

Acts records evidence of a humanly unexplainable Presence, post-Pentecost. Who is the "invisible" agent of this new Kingdom? How does He actually operate in the world? This is a mystery that defies explanation, but Acts *shows* us what happened, and gives us a working vocabulary for talking about it, words like the new organism called "the church" and the Spirit's new dynamic that "baptizes, fills, seals, adopts, engrafts, gives gifts, and brings forth fruit."

In Acts, we are witnessing the second of the 1st Century's two equally significant miracles. The opening chapters of Acts record as important a miracle as the opening chapters of the Gospels. The Incarnation of the Son's presence on earth and the Inauguration of the Spirit's presence on earth are acts of God of the same magnitude — infinite!

The believer's necessity: If the Good News stops with Incarnation of the Redeemer, we have the facts that we trust for our salvation, but not the power — the dynamic — to live our own lives 2000 years later! We might ask, "How can we be expected to keep trusting and waiting for the return of the King who has gone away for so long?" It is beyond us. Even during the 1st Century persecution, believers needed the long view. Look at Peter's first letter to the scattered believers in His day.

What assurances do you see in I Peter 1:1-12?

Yeshua knew this period of waiting would be difficult for his disciples and for future believers. *Look at the Messiah's promises as He prepared them for God's next provision and their test of faithfulness:*

John 14:16-17

John 15:26

John 16:5-15

Acts gives us historical verification of the Inauguration of this "new wine" age, sometimes called "the Age of Grace." *Look at Luke's record (in Acts 1 and 2) of this unique inaugural occurrence.*

What is the timeline from the Resurrection to Pentecost? (Acts 1:1-10; 2:1)

Where did the Inauguration happen? (Acts 2:2)

When did it happen? (Acts 2:1, 15)

What happened – in terms of the senses? (eyes, ears, nose, mouth)

How was Peter led to explain these miraculous signs, from the Old Testament? (Acts 2:14-36)

What Old Testament people did Peter quote as the basis of his explanation?
        Acts 2:16-21

Acts 2:25

Acts 2:34

The Inauguration's initial and on-going manifestation: Acts 2:33 is a very significant statement of an event that happened in Heaven, prerequisite to the arrival of the Father and Son's gift of the Spirit to earth. After that first day, what kind of things began to happen to authenticate the continuing presence of the Spirit of Christ? *Glance forward at headings in the next few chapters in your Bible (if you have a version that summarizes sections), and note various kinds of miraculous occurrences.*

The Jewish leadership did not respond warmly to this "new wine." Stephen's defense in Acts 7 skillfully summarizes the response of Israel to God's messengers. *For his frank overview of Israel's history, how was Stephen rewarded by the leadership? (Acts 7:55-60)*

The persecution of the believers that broke out after Stephen's stoning looked like bad news, but God used it to forward the message, in accordance to the risen Son's prediction in Acts 1:8.

To where did the Good News begin to spread? (See Acts 8:1, 4, 12.)

The Spirit of God chose and prepared certain leaders of the new body of Christ. God dealt with each very specifically.

How in Paul's case?

Acts 9

How in Peter's case?

Acts 10

The name "Christian" was first used at Antioch. By the time that is recorded in Acts 11:19-21, something new is happening within the body of believers. *What kind of community is the Antioch body of believers becoming?*

Soon Philip, Paul, Barnabas, Mark, Timothy, and others began to spread the word throughout Asia and Macedonia (today called Turkey and Greece.) *How did the Spirit of God continue to demonstrate His willingness to take up residence even in Gentiles, as the Gospel spread further out from Jerusalem?*

Acts 8:15-17 (in Samaria)

Acts 10:44-48 (in Caesarea)

Acts 19:1-7 (in Ephesus)

Key passages: This initial miraculous gift (mirroring the foreign languages God gave at Pentecost's Inauguration, although not the fire) was witnessed by the Jewish Apostles. This was crucial to Israelite acceptance of "half-breeds" and Gentiles into the fold of believers. Being examined by the Apostles, Peter argued, "How could I oppose God?" (Acts 11:17)

A history-changing council: Acts 15:1-35 describes how this difficult relational situation was settled. *What did the church and elders in Jerusalem decide, and why?*

Parallel with the latter chapters of Acts, the disciples were writing letters to the young churches being established in places like Rome, Corinth, Galatia, Ephesus, and Philippi. These epistles carefully explained basic facts of the gospel. They insisted that the source of every blessing bestowed upon believers was due to their being "IN Christ." They traced all God's enabling to the Spirit given to all who are "IN Christ." The pastoral letters to individuals such as Timothy and Titus prescribed how the churches were to be organized. Each letter solidified scriptural truths, followed by practical explanations of the Spirit of God's activity among them and the resulting attitudes and behavior the believers were to manifest.

Closure: Around 90 AD the Spirit concluded His later messages to the churches through the only disciple left alive, John.

Who is speaking in Revelation 1:1-3?

Note the word the glorified Lord repeats to all <u>seven</u> groups, in Revelation 2:7, 11, 17, 26; 3:5, 12, 21.

What is the burden of the Messiah's message to the seven churches?

Looking onward to the end of the New Testament: Much like the pronouncement in the 12th chapter of Daniel (verse 4 and 9) — "sealed up until the time of the end" — John's apocalyptic vision in Revelation chapters 4-22, tries to put in words what our Messiah (God's ultimate prophet, priest and king) says will happen at the end of time. (Studies 10 and 11 will focus on Revelation — when the old economy will end and the new will begin.)

From the Incarnation to the present, history has been passing through the "times of the Gentiles." The Spirit of God sustains the Kingdom throughout history, and it is He who sustains each of us throughout our personal history. He is invisible, but His presence is palpable. He is the prerequisite agent for God's glory to be seen on earth.

IN **will go on to explore specific ways this palpable presence is a reality in the believer's life.** The Spirit arranged for us to have the account of Acts for our training, understanding, and encouragement, while each of us is passing through our brief lifetime. What happened in Acts is meant to happen within each of us personally. The next few *IN* studies each focus on one aspect of *how* the Spirit of God works in the believer's life.

Our double opportunity: Let's ask the Spirit of God to awaken us to what was happening in Act's period of "inauguration," and awaken us to the Spirit's "inauguration" in our own lives.

Failure is not necessary! It is possible for any believer to be asleep spiritually, even though regenerated in God's sight. However, our God is eager for us to be awake, on our toes, receptive, responsive, cooperative, and therefore conquering and enduring. He wants us to consciously enjoy His presence. Left to ourselves, we are weak, unprotected, lethargic, defeated, and lacking in joy and hope. God wants us to rest in the knowledge of what is fully ours in Christ, and to live confidently, actually miraculously, through the power of the One Who is indwelling us! This is "living by faith"!

As we proceed through *IN*, our most basic purpose is to believe, trust, claim, and experience the work of the Spirit of God. The Godhead has provided for the life of believers in this period from Pentecost until the Lord Jesus returns. Let us not sadden our Lord, and lessen our witness, by failing to appropriate that which He has so lovingly provided.

♥ *What are my present hopes for appropriation in my own life?*

Prayer is primary! *The Apostle Paul labored tirelessly to equip those he mentored. If we become alert to Paul's burden, we will notice that prayers are sprinkled throughout his letters. Often Paul bursts into prayer as he writes. Let us apply Paul's prayer for the Ephesians to ourselves:*

> I keep asking that the God of our Lord Jesus Christ, the glorious Father, may give you the Spirit of wisdom and revelation, so that you may know him better. I pray also that the eyes of your heart may be enlightened in order that you may know the hope to which he has called you, the riches of his glorious inheritance in the saints, and his incomparably great power for us who believe.   ~ Ephesians 1:17-19a

♥ As I consider my condition before God, when did I receive the Lord Jesus Christ, and thus also received the Spirit of God?

♥ As I search my own heart, "have the eyes of my heart been opened" to these riches?

♥ What am I "tasting" of some of the hope, riches, and power Paul trusts will be the experience of every believer?

Ω

Hold on to the INAUGURATION KEY to life IN Christ

Exalted to the right hand of God, he has received from the Father the promised Holy Spirit and has poured out what you now see and hear.

Acts 2:33

Study 5

INGRAFTED

How can a Gentile enter into God's Covenant blessings?

(Drawn primarily from Romans, Galatians, and Ephesians)

Introduction: After the preceding studies on the Incarnation and Inauguration, the next few turn to various aspects of what it means to be "in Christ." Each is like one facet of a gem, reflecting one particular ray of the splendor of life "in Christ." Each is different. We begin with one that is particularly related to culture, being "ingrafted" (an alternative spelling of "engrafted").

Context: In less than 40 years, history revolved in the Ist Century around two sudden moves of God - the Incarnation of the Son in the flesh and the Inauguration of the age of the Holy Spirit! This transformation widening up to the whole world was not orchestrated by man, but was accomplished according to the counsels of the Trinity. The Jewish believers could only say, "Who were we to withstand God?" Passages in the Epistles round out Luke's historical record of this settled principle recorded in Acts. Paul's concurrent writings clarify the ramifications of the "new wine" suddenly threatening to burst the pre-Incarnation "wineskins."

God's unexpected act at Pentecost (focus of Study 4) was followed by the Spirit's initiating a new multicultural situation (focus of this Study 5). The Spirit directed Paul to use an agricultural analogy to explain the new situation: Israel's natural tree could receive wild branches (the rest of the world: "the nations," "Gentiles") by their being "grafted in." Only the Husbandman could do this grafting. Stated in a relational way, this actuality is sometimes called the doctrine of "adoption." Only the Father can adopt.

Paul's careful explanation of the Good News for both Jews and Gentiles was written to a mixed body of believers in Rome. Their future harmony hung on getting God's message right, from the beginning. The early chapters of Romans speak to both cultures about how righteousness is credited in God's eyes. The section in Romans 9, 10, and 11 focuses on the crux of the relational situation that God's "new wine" necessitated. We need to think through the implications of these immensely important three chapters that the early Christians (and we) needed to understand and accept.

God's sovereignty and man's freedom "Election" is a term used for one of the paradoxical mysteries of Scripture. Only God finds the way to bring His election and man's freedom of choice together. In our limitations, we see the two ideas as mutually exclusive. It is as if, when looking down railroad tracks, they appear quite divided, yet they merge together in infinity. The tension has sometimes been explained like this: When we choose to enter the gate of salvation, it has "Whosoever" (John 3:16) written above it. When we turn around inside and look backward, it says "Chosen before the foundation of the world." Amazing. Wonderful! Puzzling over these concepts, we can simply take God's word for both sides of the issue, and leave it with Him.

To explore the vitally important Jewish interlude in Romans 9-11, these questions may be helpful to consider:

In Romans 9:1-18, what do you glimpse of the mystery of election?

In Romans 9:19-29, what example of election does Paul cite, and what is his conclusion in 30-32?

In Romans 9:30-10:4, why did Israel fail?

In Romans 10:12, who is invited to receive the grace of God in Jesus the Messiah?

In Romans 11:5, who is "the remnant" chosen by grace?

In Romans 11:11-32, what is the relationship between Jewish and Gentile believers, between "the root and the branches"?

A crucial precedent is established: Writing to the Galatian church in Asia, Paul speaks to where they are going off track and restates the bare facts of how God brings any Jew or Gentile into His family. It was crucial for the fledgling churches to get this right. Likewise, it is crucial for any of us today to get it straight, for if we are off base, we miss redemption just as surely as the unbelieving Jews did. *Check your own mental and spiritual grasp of these key Galatian passages:*

In Galatians 2:14-16, what was the issue? (Paul even had to correct Peter in this matter.)

In Galatians 3:6-14, how does Paul appeal to Abraham's precedent for "justification"?

God's *promises* endure; the *Law* was temporary. The historical order of revelation is important. Calling attention to the step by step progression of God's plan of redemption, Paul stresses vital facts in Galatians.

For Discussion:

🕯 From Galatians 3:15-29, which "economy" trumps the other, in God's sight?

🕯 Exactly who was the promise given to? Note verses 16-17.

🕯 What, then, was the purpose of the law?

♥ According to Galatians 3:29, are you "Abraham's seed"?

♥ If you are, what is also yours, and on what basis?

Note the code word "circumcision" — i.e. Israel's separation unto God. "Circumcision" is a term of deep significance to the "sons of Abraham." Given as a sign of God's covenant with Abraham's descendants (Genesis 17:10-14), circumcision was performed on a hidden organ, the organ of reproduction — of genealogy — the "begats." But Moses and the prophets called the Israelites to task for their often superficial identification with their God, chiding them for having "uncircumcised hearts" — as in Leviticus 26:40-42, and Jeremiah 4:4. In Deuteronomy 30:6, God promised to "circumcise the hearts and ears" of those who returned to the Lord.

After the Messiah came, how did "circumcision" apply? Because circumcision is a usual health practice in western society today, we do not realize how loaded with meaning the terms "circumcised" and "uncircumcised" were in the 1st Century. The mark of "belonging" to the covenant community was circumcision. The pagan nations were generally uncircumcised. The Letters to the fledgling congregations refer frequently to this issue. *Examples:*

Romans 2:29 Who actually accomplishes spiritual circumcision?

Philippians 3:3 What is true "circumcision" really about?

Colossians 2:11-12 How is the believer "spiritually circumcised"?

God's judgment on this issue at the time of the founding of the church is summarized in Galatians 5:6 and 6:15. While circumcision practices have changed over the years, what is the principle at the center of this difficult question, in Paul's day?

For Discussion:

☖ *What "marks of acceptance" might believers in New Testament times today wrongly substitute for the "circumcision" mark?*

☖ *What am I counting on as my mark of "belonging" to the Covenant people?*

Sealed! All God's promises are "Yes!" in Christ, as Paul affirms in II Corinthians 1:20-22. God has given His people a "deposit" in time, to be made good when the hour of fulfillment comes. *Examining II Corinthians 1:20-22, consider:*

What three guarantees are given to believers?

In contrast to circumcision, are they visible? Who sees this "seal"?

In Ephesians 1:13-14, God's "seal" is identified to be _____!

The Spirit of God supervised the circumcision issue in the Ist Century. The "Judaizers" were checked. However, false relational attitudes that grew during the 4th Century have plagued Christendom. The "Gentilizers" began to triumph. The Church has inherited seeds of Jewish and Gentile misunderstanding since the time of Constantine in the 300s AD. Although Constantine has been credited as the emperor whose favor opened up the Roman Empire to Christianity, Constantine also set up anti-Jewish policies that have been much used by the ancient enemy of the Chosen People. The seeds of "replacement theology" were sown — that the Church had replaced Israel, inheriting her blessings.

The fact of Jewish suffering: Imagine what it would have meant to Jewish families in Rome (a mixture of people who did or did not accept Jesus as the Messiah) for the government to forbid any Jewish person to celebrate Passover and other Feasts and Holy Days, and in some places, even the Sabbath. If disobeying, they could be exiled and their property confiscated. They were not given equal civil rights. They were not allowed to intermarry with Christians. Over the centuries, in various countries they were given only three options:

conversion, exile, or death. The Crusades are well known, but there were many other periods of increased Jewish persecution, right up to the Holocaust.

Error grew! Some Christian denominations today still persist in the long-inherited doctrine that the Church completely replaced Israel — sometimes called "supercessionism." Through this Replacement Theology, the Jewish community was crossed off in a way that led to centuries of injustice and persecution. It influences attitudes and outcomes today.

No, let's be clear, the New Covenant was given to Israel. By God's grace, Gentile believers who were "grafted" into Israel simply became fellow-heirs with the Covenant People. These Old and New Testament Scriptures are very clear: (Jeremiah wrote about 600 BC.) (Notice that in the 1st Century AD, Hebrews 8:8-12 is quoting Jeremiah 31:31-34.) *Compare these Scriptures:*

Jeremiah 31:31 With whom is the New Covenant to be established?

Hebrews 8:6-7 Why was a new covenant needed?

Hebrews 9:15 What had to take place to put the New Covenant into action?

Well then, how can Gentiles be included in the New Covenant? By being ingrafted - or in other words of Scripture, being "adopted," "included," "accepted" as sons and daughters of Abraham — by faith! How amazing, how kind, to be allowed full citizenship with the Chosen People! Yet this was God's purpose from the beginning.

Review the following Scriptures that indicate God's heart for gathering in the whole world (i.e. "the nations" — the Gentiles):

Genesis 12:3b

Genesis 18:18

Psalm 96:3

Isaiah 42:6

Ezekiel 36:23

Haggai 2:7

Believing Gentiles become "accepted in the Beloved." Although always in God's plan, this mystery came to the light after the Messiah's work of salvation had been completed. *See these clear statements of the mysterious but wonderful way our Father worked it out, when "the times of the Gentiles" arrived:*

From Galatians 3:26-29, what distinctions are nullified? What is the the inheritance of ALL who are "in Christ Jesus"?

From Ephesians 2:11-14, how does Paul show the "before and after" condition of Gentiles who believe?

From Ephesians 2:14-18, what was it that reconciled Jews and Gentiles to become "one new man"?

From Ephesians 2:19-21, what status have believing Gentiles been given "in Christ"? How integral is their role?

Gentile Christians owe the Jewish patriarchs great respect and consideration. Recalling all they have given the world, Paul poured out his heartbreak over Israel:

> *Theirs is the adoption as sons; theirs the divine glory, the covenants, the receiving of the law, the temple worship and the promises. Theirs are the patriarchs, and from them is traced the human ancestry of Christ, who is God over all, forever praised! Amen.*   ~ Romans 9:4-5

Gentile Christians rightfully identify with these patriarchs who have nurtured and taught "wild branches" the ways of God, and the history of His interactions with them. Over and over again God has vowed His love for Israel, even in her unfaithfulness, and has promised to bless those who bless her:

> *I have loved you with an everlasting love.*   ~ Jeremiah 31:3a

> *I will bless those who bless you…*   ~ Genesis 12:3

We are sobered as we compare the graciousness of the Jewish believers toward receiving Gentiles at the Jerusalem Council reported in Acts 15 with the ungracious Gentile treatment of Jewish believers over the centuries. Constantine put up "roadblocks to redemption," in the words of a leader among Messianic believers in Christ, Jonathan Bernis in his 2008 *Jewish Voice Today,* "Roadblocks to Redemption" article (in the September/October issue). These roadblocks set up in Rome (and elsewhere over the centuries) effectively smothered and exiled Jewish Christians, persecuted the whole Jewish community, and left unbelieving Jews isolated and ignored. In our times, Satan's use of the Holocaust almost stamped out God's covenant people and Israel's faith in her God.

We live in exciting times, however, on the edge of reconciliation. The number of Jewish people who are believing in Jesus as the Messiah (in Israel and throughout the wider world) is growing exponentially in our generation. They prefer to call themselves "Messianic Jews," because the term "Christian" is so deeply stained with Jewish blood, in their community's eyes. This believing remnant (Romans 9:27 and 11:5) is insisting on being accepted as fully Jewish by Israel, and as fully Christian by the Church worldwide. In fact, we live at a time when a call has actually gone out for "a Second Jerusalem Council" — to recognize the Church's error and redirect the course of events that God's enemy has so long orchestrated.

All tribes and nations are envisioned at the Throne in Revelation 5:9. God is being worshipped in diversity. While He has constituted believing Jews and Gentiles as "one man in Christ," that oneness does not nullify the distinction of tribes and tongues, including Israel. Messianic Jewish believers beg Gentiles, as did Paul in Romans 10, to care about the message getting to Israelites who are languishing in unbelief. They too can only be "justified" in the same way Gentiles must be, by faith — as was our mutual father Abraham. We often take this passage in Romans 10:8-13 out of its Jewish context. Are Jewish people not included in "anyone" and "everyone"?

"Israel has experienced a hardening in part until the full number of the Gentiles has come in," says the "Hebrew of Hebrews" in Romans 11:25b. In this period, Gentile believers were supposed to make Israel "envious" (Romans 11:11, 14). Perhaps in these closing days, the Church can be reawakened to her calling to winsomely share joy and hope in the Son of David, the rejected Cornerstone, into whom she has been graciously ingrafted.

We live at an unprecedented time of "softening" in the Jewish community worldwide. Consider this openness in conjunction with Christ's promise in Matthew 24:14.

For Discussion:

🕯 *What might be the implication for us, seeing the convergence of today's softening and Jesus' promise in Matthew 24:14?*

♥ *If I am a non-Jewish believer in the Messiah, how might I better appreciate the gift of having been ingrafted into the family of God?*

♥ *If I have largely ignored the position in which Israel has been placed by Christendom, what might be my response now as I talk with the God of Abraham, Isaac, and Jacob in prayer?*

Prayer: *Let's pray the concluding words of the teaching on Israel in Romans 11:33-36:*

> Oh, the depth of the riches of the wisdom and knowledge of God! How unsearchable his judgments, and his paths beyond tracing out! "Who has known the mind of the Lord? Or who has been his counselor?" Who has ever given to God, that God should repay him? For from him and through him and to him are all things. To him be the glory forever! Amen.

Ω

Hold on to the INGRAFTED KEY to being IN Christ

If some of the branches have been broken off, and you, though a wild olive shoot, have been grafted in among the others and now share in the nourishing sap from the olive root, do not boast over those branches. If you do, consider this: You do not support the root, but the root supports you.

Romans 11:17-18

Study 6

IMPUTED

How can any son or daughter of Adam be saved from judgment and accepted as 'righteous' in God's sight?

(Drawn largely from Romans)

Introduction: Human beings seem consistently to long for acceptance from their god, whatever "god" they focus upon. False religions and secular formulas are flawed. How the God of Jesus the Christ thinks, and how the world thinks, are so opposite that even the Biblically-literate believer can struggle with this very basic need and drive in life. God has gone to great pains to make this issue clear to us, for our sake and for His.

*First, a definition: What does "impute" mean? (Notice that in this study's title, the "in" prefix is spelled "im." Why? In English, an "in" before the letters b, m, and p are changed to "im" for easier pronunciation.) To "impute" means "to charge or credit another with, to attribute, to count as, or to ascribe vicariously." What the King James Version translates "impute," other versions translate "reckon" or "count." The term expresses a life-and-death transaction. God imputes righteousness (i.e. credits it) to those who trust in His Son's sin payment.

Context: Sons and daughters of Adam, sinners all, labor under the sentence of death brought in by the Fall. From the beginning, Genesis 3 tells us, God promised that a "seed of a woman" would finally crush the Serpent's head. God provided a way to obtain righteousness (rightness with God), but this has been a thorny issue between God and man throughout history. From Cain's self-righteous offering in the opening chapters of Genesis to today, humanity has stumbled over this issue.

Why is this matter of how to obtain "righteousness" still important to us today? Because our own salvation depends upon it! *Look at what it meant for Israel to miss the mark on this account:*

Romans 10:1-4

♥ *So how serious will it be, if I too, seek to establish my own righteousness, and miss the mark on this "imputed righteousness" issue?*

Abraham is our Old Testament model for "getting it right," and it is to his example that the New Testament appeals. Let us begin with Abraham's experience, the Biblical prototype for God's requirement for man's righteousness. In brief, although Abram and Sarai are childless and well past the years of childbearing, God gives Abram a promise of a son, necessitating a miraculous birth. Abram believes, but errs as time goes on, fathering Ishmael (Genesis 16). The promise is repeated (Genesis 17:1-10) and Abraham's descendants are given the mark of circumcision. Again the promise is given, this time through angels (Genesis 18:1-15). Finally, the child of the promise is born, Isaac (Genesis 21:1-6). God makes a sovereign decision about the *line of the promise*, saying, "...it is through Isaac that your offspring will be reckoned" (Genesis 21:12b). Astoundingly, in Genesis 22 God requires the sacrifice of this father's only son. Why? If we can grasp the answer, we glimpse the pre-figured mystery of salvation through the sacrifice the Father and the Son made on Mt. Moriah 2000 years later.

God's way of righteousness remains the same through both Old and New Testaments, and today. *Let us ponder some of the significant principles mediated to us through the story of Abraham, "father of the faithful."*

From the key verse, Genesis 15:6, what did Abraham do?

Going to the New Testament, trace these ongoing affirmations of the principle Abraham's faith demonstrated, and how it applies to us as well:

Romans 4:3, 20-25

Galatians 3:6-7

David lived a thousand years after Abraham, but he understood God's view of righteousness. It is from David that we get the classic quotation about "imputed" righteousness. In his Psalm 32:1-2, the KJV says,

> *"Blessed is he whose transgression is forgiven, whose sin is covered. Blessed is the man unto whom the LORD imputeth not iniquity, and in whose spirit there is no guile."*

In the NIV it is translated,

> *"Blessed is he whose transgressions are forgiven, whose sins are covered. Blessed is the man whose sin the Lord does not count against him, and in whose spirit is no deceit."*

Another thousand years later, Paul instructs the early believers using Abraham's example in the books of Romans and Galatians, both of which refer back to Abraham in Genesis.

Today, this same issue cuts the rug out from under our pre-conceived notions about how to be accepted by God. "Surely our good upbringing, surely our good works, surely our piety, surely our sincere efforts deserve to earn us acceptance as righteous," we imagine. The human tendency is to do anything but admit failure to earn God's favor on our own.

Although the world's mistaken viewpoint is probably deep in our own subconscious, God's corrected approach is carefully put forth in His word. The Gospel of the Lord Jesus the Christ is spelled out step by step in the book of Romans. Paul makes the <u>bad</u> news clear in Romans 2 and 3, before he gives the <u>good</u> news. Mankind faces God's wrath for sin. Repentance is crucial.

> *But because of your stubbornness and your unrepentant heart, you are storing up wrath against yourself of the day of God's wrath, when his righteous judgment will be revealed.*   ~ Romans 2:5

Speaking to the Jewish community who had relied on keeping the Law, Paul says,

> *"Therefore no one will be declared righteous in his sight by observing the law; rather, through the law we become conscious of sin."* ~ Romans 3:20

In summary, the whole world stands guilty before God.

The Bad News sounds hopeless, but we ask with Paul,

> *"What then shall we say that Abraham, our forefather, discovered in this matter?"*   ~ Romans 4:1

The Good News is truly good, if we understand the only alternative! God's provision is so important for each of us, and for the whole world, that His answer to our predicament needs to be made indelible in our minds and hearts.

"Imputing" requires two parties, the giver and receiver. God's part is to offer this gracious gift, ours is to receive it in the way He authorizes. He has made both sides of this transaction clear.

God's part: Our Maker told our original parents the choice to sin would cause death. In spite of their tragic choice, in His love He devised a way for them to escape their just penalty. He prepared that way carefully over the centuries, and even gave Abraham a foretaste of what the Father and Son were going to do about it, on Mt. Moriah.

Man's part: We the accused must go before the Judge, and there is no doubt as to our guilt. If God were to be true to His character, He must judge justly. Where does that leave man as he stands before the Judge? A key element in great news the early believers announced was that Jesus was to be the Father's appointed judge.

Consider the majesty ascribed to the Risen Christ as the judge of all mankind:

Acts 10:42-43

Acts 17:30-31

At the Messiah's first coming, the Father and Son settled this seemingly unsolvable predicament of the human race. A best-loved Bible verse summarizes their plan:

> *For God so loved the world that he gave his one and only Son, that whoever believes in him shall not perish but have eternal life."*   ~ John 3:16

When the time was right, the incarnate Son came to settle the sin debt of humanity, humbling Himself even to the extent of death at the hands of men. Jesus' vicarious atonement was God's gracious solution!

At His second coming, we are warned, He must judge the world. Between His two comings, humanity is given the gracious offer of accepting God's forgiveness. This grace is offered in a way that shows us the justice and love of God wedded together. A just payment for sin is truly made, but it is paid for by God Himself.

Imagine yourself in a court scene at the time of Judgment. You stand guilty before the Judge. You have taken God's word for it, that the Savior really did pay your debt on Calvary. Hear the Judge pronounce your sentence: "Paid in full. Forgiven!" As the gavel comes down with finality, see the nail prints in the Judge's hand.

Jesus is both Savior and Lord. Now is the time for His saving work to be proclaimed, before He returns as King of kings and Lord of lords. Jesus' last words to the church in the book of Revelation assure us of His authority:

"I am the First and the Last. I am the Living One; I was dead, and behold I am alive for ever and ever! And I hold the keys of death and Hades."
~ Revelation 1:17b-18

This message resounded across the Roman Empire in the 1st Century as the early disciples urged the next generation to stay faithful to their message:

In the presence of God and of Christ Jesus, who will judge the living and the dead, and in view of his appearing and his kingdom, I give you this charge: Preach the Word; be prepared in season and out of season; correct, rebuke and encourage — with great patience and careful instruction. For the time will come when men will not put up with sound doctrine. ~ II Timothy 4:1-3a

Yes, we ourselves live at a time when many "do not put up with sound doctrine," but that does not lessen our calling to teach the truth.

God wants us to understand His truly good news. Righteousness before Him may be transacted by faith. *Let these Romans passages marinate in your mind and soul:*

God's statement of the principle in Romans 3:21-31

Abraham's concrete example in Romans 4:5, 11, 21-25

The role of the 1st and 2nd Adam, and the Law, explained in
Romans 5:12-21

Our forgiveness, hope, and joy come on the same basis as found in
Romans. We too can only (and thankfully) be justified by the blood
of our Savior, whose death substituted for our own, cancelling the
charge against us, and crediting us with "paid in full."

> *Since we have now been justified by his blood, how much more shall we be*
> *saved from God's wrath through him! For if, when we were God's enemies, we*
> *were reconciled to him through the death of his Son, how much more, having*
> *been reconciled, shall we be saved through his life! Not only is this so, but*
> *we also rejoice in God through our Lord Jesus Christ, through whom we have*
> *now received reconciliation.* ~ Romans 5:9

Perhaps our pride cries out, "But why can't I earn my own payment
for my sin debt?" *Scripture makes clear what I do earn and what God
wants to give me:*

In Romans 6:23, what is my payment and what is God's gift?

From Ephesians 2:8-10 what, instead of my works, brings me
salvation?
And where do my works fit in?

Strength **of faith is not our need; it is faith's** *focus.* **How did this**
astounding event (passed on to us by Genesis 22:1-19) reveal the
focus of Abraham's faith? Hebrews 11:17-19 gives us a clue about this
almost unbelievable test. *What do the two passages taken together
indicate?*

"Having faith" is not an end in itself. That is a sterile "formula." *Saving faith* is placed in the *Person behind the promise,* in God Himself.

If my pride still cries out, let me ask the Spirit of God to speak to me through an Old Covenant preview of the 2nd Adam's work on my behalf.

What stands out to me in Isaiah 53, especially in verses 4-6?

How to be redeemed is the burden of the Good News. What the early apostles proclaimed applies to us as well:

> *That if you confess with your mouth, "Jesus is Lord," and believe in your heart that God raised him from the dead, you will be saved. For it is with your heart that you believe and are justified, and it is with your mouth that you confess and are saved. As the Scripture says, "Anyone who trusts in him will never be put to shame." For there is no difference between Jew and Gentile — the same Lord is Lord of all and richly blesses all who call on him, for, "Everyone who calls on the name of the Lord will be saved."* ~ Romans 10:9-13

♥ *So, on whose effort does God say anyone's salvation depends? Does that bring forth resentment or thankfulness in me?*

♥ *Do I count myself to be "imputed" (counted) into that completed payment — the finished work of Christ?*

The Great Exchange: "Imputed" is a major aspect of the marvelous gift from God to man called "grace." Imputed righteousness is not just divine assistance toward goodness, it is total rescue. This is one of the most amazing exchanges ever accomplished:

> *God made him who had no sin to be sin for us, so that in him we might become the righteousness of God.*   ~ II Corinthians 5:21

A well-worded summary points out that "The Lord Jesus died a death we could not survive to pay a debt we could not afford." Now that's *grace!*

What would the world *pay* for that which is a *gift* to the believer? If my debt has been paid and I am credited with Jesus' righteousness, incredible peace can be mine.

"Therefore" (first word) introduces what two reasons for this peace?

Romans 5:1-2

Romans 8:1-2

♥ *How much am I consciously enjoying the above "therefores" that naturally follow, if I have accepted the Good News in Christ?*

♥ *What might II Corinthians 5:16-21 suggest I am called to DO in response to the acceptance God imputes to me by His grace?*

Prayer:

Dear Father, Where am I in all this? What do I need to pray?

Ω

Hold on to the IMPUTED KEY to being IN Christ

⌐━┳

Consider Abraham: "He believed God, and it was credited to him as righteousness." Understand, then, that those who believe are children of Abraham. The Scripture foresaw that God would justify the Gentiles by faith, and announced the gospel in advance to Abraham. "All nations will be blessed through you." So those who have faith are blessed along with Abraham, the man of faith.

Galatians 3:6-9

Study 7

INCLUDED

Into what position does God bring every one who is 'in Christ'?

(Drawn largely from Ephesians, Philippians, and Colossians)

Introduction: *Yeshua*'s prayer to the Father the night before He gave Himself, asked that "they may be one as we are one, I in them and you in me. May they be brought to complete unity to let the world know that you sent me and have loved them even as you have loved me." Such unity was humanly impossible, yet God accomplished it. Letters to the early churches are addressed "to the saints <u>in</u> Christ Jesus," and "to the church <u>in</u> God the Father and the Lord Jesus Christ." Do we hear echoes of Jesus' High Priestly prayer?

Context: Israel in the desert after the Exodus was totally cared for by God. Everyone in the covenant community was embraced in His care. Pagan Gentiles were outside this community, being "strangers to the covenant of promise." Study 5 focused on God's gracious ingrafting of believing Gentiles into the new covenant community. This study focuses on God's bounty poured out upon everyone who believes, whether Jew or Gentile, without exception.

God can transform people from "have-nots to haves." Not a fairytale of Cinderella and her Prince, this possibility of rescue is God's non-fiction truth. The Spirit of God transfers those who receive the Lord from their former condition of wandering lost outside of Christ to being found securely in Him. This mysterious "inclusion" is revealed especially in the letters to the Ephesians, Philippians, and Colossians. Miraculous God-ordained relationships are set forth, "you in Christ" and "Christ in you."

According to Ephesians 2:1-3, and 11-13, what had been the Ephesians' condition when they were unbelievers?

From Philippians 2:1-2, what are natural outgrowths of being "united with Christ"?

From Colossians 2:13-15, how did Jesus triumph over sin, to make possible the destiny and inheritance of all believers?

This being "made alive" includes complete forgiveness — the cancelling of all our sins by Christ's work on the cross!

The unity of the forgiven, the Body of Christ, is based on being gathered together in "one baptism." Believers all have "one Lord, one faith, and one baptism" (Ephesians 4:5). Baptism is used in a number of ways in the Scriptures. This reference is not to water baptism, but to the baptism poured out at Pentecost, a baptism into which all believers ("the church") are spiritually immersed. John the Baptizer made the distinction:

> *I baptize you with water for repentance. But after me will come one who is more powerful than I, whose sandals I am not fit to carry. He will baptize you with the Holy Spirit and with fire.*   ~ Matthew 3:11

Just before the risen Christ's ascension, He promised the arrival of a baptism: "For John baptized with water, but in a few days you will be baptized with the Holy Spirit" (Acts 1:5). The day of Pentecost, Peter addressed the crowd quoting Joel's prediction of a time when the Spirit would be poured out. "This is that," Peter announced. He traced the timing of this baptism to the exaltation of the Son that had just taken place in heaven: "Exalted to the right hand of God, he has received from the Father the promised Holy Spirit and has poured out what you now see and hear" (Acts 2:33). The Son's exaltation in heaven was followed by the Spirit's deployment to earth!

Water baptism is different. It is a visible symbol of the believer's union with Christ. This physical demonstration is a metaphor for the believer's "inclusion" in Christ's own death, burial, and resurrection. Water baptism acts out the believer's new position in God's sight. The ceremony pictures two sides of a coin: the believer's chosen identification with the Savior, and God's act of "identifying" the believer completely with Jesus' finished work.

From spiritual rags to riches (Philippians 4:13)! One aspect after another is included in what becomes true of one who is "united" with Christ (Philippians 2:1). The basis of "inclusion" is explained especially in the opening chapters of Ephesians and Colossians. Its basis rests in Christ Himself. *What do these Scriptures say about Jesus?*

Colossians 1:17-18

Colossians 2:3

Colossians 2:9

Everything the believer has is "in Christ." The Chinese Bible teacher, Watchman Nee, in *The Normal Christian Life* (on pages 31-32), illustrated the position of the believer by placing a piece of paper in a book. Wherever you take the book (the Lord Jesus), the paper (the believer) is "in" the book. In God's view unbound by time, the eternal facts of the Savior's life are eternally accomplished. God chooses to *include* the believer in the Son's past, present, and future history. The Spirit of God affirms this over and over.

To reiterate, from what state to what state do the Scriptures trace the "history" of the believer who is "in Christ"—united with the Savior? There are many events in Christ's experience that His people are "credited" with, as well. *Write in the references where these statements can be found from Galatians 2:20; Ephesians 2:5-6; 3:6; Galatians 3:29; Colossians 2:12-13.*

_____crucified

_____dead

_____buried

_____raised

_____made alive

_____seated

_____made heirs

♥ *Do you consider yourself to be included in these seven transformations?*

Romans focuses on the depth of this union in terms of death and resurrection. *See how Paul applies these truths to believers in Romans 6:1-14:*

What does water baptism symbolize?

How thoroughly does God say we are united with Christ?

What is our challenge to believe and activate?

We may respond to Romans 6 with "Unbelievable!" or "Humanly impossible!" Yes, both. Yet God says that in His sight, this "inclusion" is true of the believer, and we cannot but believe God. Once we believe these truths, our choice is whether or not to "reckon" them to our own account, as intended by the Giver.

Reckoning: "Reckon" is an old word for "count." Reckon is an exact term, meaning to strictly balance an account, as in banking. We can "count" on God to have made the deposit He says He has. Our challenge is to believe Him, and to draw on that account. The deep well of Romans 6 needs the Spirit of God to interpret His truth to the believer, and once "reckoned," to make that truth real in daily life.

The vital connection between truth and life: "Therefore," "Since," and "So then" are transitions in Ephesians 5:1, Colossians 2:6; 3:1, etc. These words are signals meaning "because this, then that" — i.e. "Since 2 plus 2 makes 4, then count on that fact and incorporate it into your math." In similar fashion, the New Testament Letters usually first state objective truths, and then expand on the practical implications of those facts for the believers' lives. Notice how these transitional words introduce the personal application chapters in Ephesians 4:1--6:20 and Colossians 2:6-4:6.

This two-part order is as if to say, "Since God has done all this for us — included us and provided in every way for us — then let us live His life out!" We are fully resourced! The latter portion of the letters go on to spell out all sorts of issues in everyday life — issues of morality, unity, stability, maturity, marriage, family relationships, Body life, spiritual warfare, worship, and more. Godly living is preceded by godly believing.

Success in application is not based upon the striver's strength of will, but depends on the reality of the promises being claimed. Therefore Paul prayed fervently for the Ephesian believers to experience the enlivening ministry of...

> ...*the Spirit of wisdom and revelation, so that ... the eyes of your heart may be* <u>*enlightened*</u> *in order that you may know the hope to which he has called you, the riches of his glorious inheritance in the saints, and his incomparably great power for us who believe.*   ~ Ephesians 1:17-19

Without the Spirit's enlightenment, we, like the Ephesians, are all like blind beggars.

Scripture tells me that the believer is integrally included in the finished work of Christ! Will I actively trust (reckon) this or not? First I must <u>know</u>, and then I must <u>reckon</u>, in that order. "So then faith cometh by hearing, and hearing by the word of God" (Romans 10:17 KJV). We need daily immersion in God's truth. The deeper I know, the more I can reckon.

♥ *Do I reckon myself to actually be crucified, dead, buried, raised, seated, and made an heir with Christ?*

♥ *Am I relaxing gratefully before God, knowing my position is secure, in His sight? (Remember, position and condition are two different things.)*

♥ *How is my* <u>*faith*</u> *impacted by the knowledge of my being included in all the wealth and privilege that is the Son's?*

♥ *How is my daily <u>living</u> affected by knowing I am included so totally in Christ? Examples?*

Praying Scripture: *God speaks to us through His word. We speak to Him through prayer. Both sides of this heavenly conversation depend on the Spirit's mediation. It is He who brings our communication alive, both directions. As you use Biblical prayers, savor and claim each thought for yourself. You are one among the whole body of accepted and marvelously included children of God. Listen intently to the Spirit praying through Paul in Colossians 1:9-14:*

> For this reason, since the day we heard about you, we have not stopped praying for you and asking God to fill you with the knowledge of his will through all spiritual wisdom and understanding. And we pray this in order that you may live a life worthy of the Lord and may please him in every way: bearing fruit in every good work, growing in the knowledge of God, being strengthened with all power according to his glorious might so that you may have great endurance and patience, and joyfully giving thanks to the Father, who has qualified you to share in the inheritance of the saints in the kingdom of light. For he has rescued us from the dominion of darkness and brought us into the kingdom of the Son he loves, in whom we have redemption, the forgiveness of sins.

Ω

Hold on to the INCLUDED KEY to being IN Christ:

And you also were included in Christ when you heard the word of truth, the gospel of your salvation. Having believed, you were marked in him with a seal, the promised Holy Spirit, who is a deposit guaranteeing our inheritance until the redemption of those who are God's possession — to the praise of his glory.

Ephesians 1:13-14

Study 8

INDWELT

Why do the reborn have resources the un-regenerated lack?

(Drawn principally from the Letters)

Introduction: *Yeshua* looked like any son of Adam, yet He was the Anointed One, anointed by the very Spirit of God. He appeared limited like any human, yet He moved in the power of the Spirit. He was different from ordinary mortals, for He was filled with all the fullness of God. Amazingly, He delights to put His spiritual offspring in that same position, anointing them and filling them with the very presence of God. Do we, can we, believe this?

Context: Each facet of God's life in Christ gleams with a different hue, so to speak. Just as God reveals Himself through name after name, so also His gifts to His children can be called by one name after another. Each describes a different aspect. The Father chooses to <u>ingraft</u> a non-Israelite into His covenant people; He <u>imputes</u> the Son's righteousness to the believer's account; and then the Father and the Son send the Spirit to <u>indwell</u> the believer.

This "indwelling" was something new. It was related to the Spirit's presence from the beginning of Genesis. Throughout the Old Testament, the third Person of the Trinity would come upon Old Testament people to equip them for special tasks. The Spirit anointed kings, prophets, and priests to enable them supernaturally for some calling. The New Testament makes a prepositional distinction between how the Spirit related to the covenant people before and after Pentecost. Before, He was "with" them. After, He came "into" them. (John 7:37-39 clearly explains the progression.)

See this distinction that Jesus made as He prepared the disciples for the Spirit's coming in this new way:

John 14:16-17

John 15:26-27

John 16:7-15

This "in-ness" of the Spirit is the way the early believers spoke of their relationship with Him. *Consider these examples:*

Romans 8:10-11

II Corinthians 13:5

Galatians 2:20

Ephesians 3:16-17

I John 4:4

Colossians 1:25-27

"Christ in you, the hope of glory" is the key to what humanity is hungering for — intimate fellowship with God, and hope for eternity. Taken together, they constitute both temporal and eternal life with Him!

At Pentecost, the dynamism of God was turned loose! The Spirit's indwelling demonstrates the *dynamic* aspect of life "in Christ." How could the early Christians presume to literally possess the presence of the Holy Spirit? This claim was not born of human philosophy. They whole thing came as a total surprise. As He was about to ascend, Jesus promised that power was about to come upon them (Acts 1:8). On the Day of Pentecost, God suddenly poured out the Spirit, demonstrating His presence at that unique moment related to the Son's glorification (Acts 2:33). Immediately God continued to demonstrate this presence in miraculous ways. No one was more amazed than the believers themselves. Imagine being among them when the power of God was being mediated through them to heal the sick, cast out unclean spirits, and even to raise the dead! No one was more convinced of the power that was passing through them than they were. They looked so ordinary, yet what was happening was extraordinary.

When the very presence of God indwells humans today, how do believers "look" different from "ordinary mortals"? Living in their mortal physical bodies, they may not look distinctive (except in the eyes and turn of mouth perhaps), but their capacity will be amazingly "resourced" to say the least!

These resources that the Father delights to give to His children are often referred to in Scripture as "fruit" or "gifts." The Christian community often loses sight of the Father when receiving His benefits, arguing over them competitively, like children at Christmas. Their purpose is quite wonderful — to glorify the Father, and to bless the whole Body of Christ. They are meant to bless the world as well.

Fruit is the natural product of a tree. A vine does not grunt and strain to produce grapes; the fruit is a natural product of the sap within the vine. *Yeshua* described this process in a simple but profound way. *In these verses, who is the gardener, who the vine, who the sap, who the branch? What is the purpose of the fruit?*

John 15:1-8

Gifts are gifts. They are neither earned nor chosen by the receiver. The gifts of the Spirit depend upon God's sovereign choice, freely bestowed, to be received thankfully, trusting that the Father knows which gifts are best for each of His children. While their possession should not be a matter of competition, Paul does advise his congregation to "follow the way of love and eagerly desire spiritual gifts, especially the gift of prophecy." The Spirit's special gifts to the Body <u>in</u> whom Christ dwells is the focus of I Corinthians 12, and Ephesians 4.

The outcropping (or appropriation) of these resources is called "being filled with the Spirit." Although the redeemed have all of Him, He usually does not have all of us. This "filling" (<u>in</u> not just <u>with</u>) was powerfully demonstrated at Pentecost, and then continued.

See the progression:

Acts 2:4

Acts 4:8

Ephesians 5:18

What part can the believer take in activating the "fullness of the Spirit"? We can want this selfishly, but we can also want it for God's glory. *Yeshua* could say so much in such few words. As He prepared the disciples for the Spirit's coming, He described a process their attitude and obedience could enhance. What can be a trigger to increase our "fullness"? Jesus explained this during His last night with them. The King James Version uses "make our abode" and RSV uses "manifest" for what the NIV translates "show."

> *He who <u>has</u> my commandments and <u>keeps</u> them, he it is who <u>loves</u> me; and he who loves me will <u>be loved</u> by my Father, and I will love him, and <u>manifest</u> myself to him.*   ~ John 14:21 (RSV)

Someone has pictured the momentum of this promise as moving around the points of a star. *On the diagram below, place an underlined verb (from John 14:21 above) on each point.*

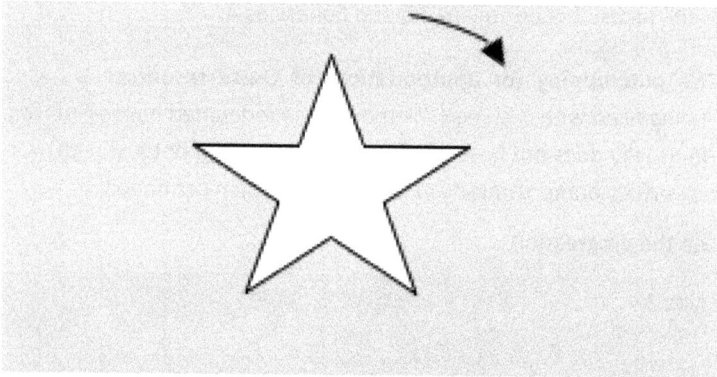

What follows what, and what brings more of what? What does the star reveal about the deeper unfolding of our Lord's love, and the response of the loved one? Jesus shows the key to be love-engendered-<u>obedience</u>, i.e. wanting what God wants. Somehow obedience causes God to reveal Himself, which spurs on our love for Him the more, which spurs on our obedience to Him the more, which spurs on His further revelation to the seeking heart, anew. This momentum can be continual in the believer's life when obedience is the loved one's response.

Who can do this in us? Jesus deployed the Spirit of God to be the agent of making our Lord real to us.

He will bring glory to me by taking from what is mine and making it known to you. All that belongs to the Father is mine. That is why I said the Spirit will take from what is mine and make it known to you.   ~ John 16:14-15

♥ *Do I recognize the Presence of the Holy Spirit within me?*

♥ *Is this a matter of fact, of faith, or of feeling?*

The best answer is all three, but their order is crucial. Watchman Nee in his book *The Normal Christian Life* (on pages 55-56) said the difficulty with maintaining the Christian life is like that of three men walking along on top of a high wall. If FAITH turns around and looks at FEELING, the two may well fall off of the wall. If FAITH keeps his eyes on FACT, with FEELING following along, they can proceed without accident. The fact of what is ours in Christ needs to be the focus of our faith. Feelings are best disciplined to follow behind faith, rather than grabbing the leadership in a direction that can well distract or manipulate.

This meditation and prayer of evangelist F. B. Meyer may be a help as you consider the fact of the Spirit's presence in the believer's core:

It is my confident belief that there is not a single man or woman who believes in Christ who has not Christ in the heart. But remember, that as the heavy veil hid the holy of holies from the holy place, so Jesus Christ may be in your heart; but because you have never recognized that He is there, because you have made no use of His presence there, because you have been unbelieving, and maybe indolent to respond to His appeal, though He has been in your heart ever since you were regenerate, His presence has been hidden from your eyes; it has been veiled. I pray God that the two hands that rent the veil of the temple in twain from the top to the bottom, may rend the veil in your inner life that the Christ who is there may be revealed in you.

[F. B. Meyer (1848-1929) quoted by J. Oswald Sanders in *Christ Indwelling and Enthroned*, 1949, page 25.]

Yes, the <u>revelation</u> of His Presence makes a great difference in the believer's life. Scripture insists that the third Person of the Trinity indwells every believer, saying,

"And if anyone does not have the Spirit of Christ, he does not belong to Christ."   ~ Romans 8:9b

The Spirit invests us with power, but He <u>is</u> a Person. He wills, acts, communicates, teaches, comforts, and fellowships with His people. His power and His prophecies can be quenched or despised (I Thessalonians 5:19, KJV).

"Fullness" is the need. The question is not whether a believer is indwelt, but rather how fully the Spirit is allowed to flood the life and overflow into the world. *Yeshua* spoke powerfully about this. Yearly at the Feast of Tabernacles, a "water ceremony" was enacted before the covenant community. The Lord used that dramatic moment when water was being poured out from the ceremonial pitcher to reveal what He and the Spirit longed to pour out, to God's glory.

On the last great day of the Feast, Jesus stood and said in a loud voice, "If anyone is thirsty; let him come to me and drink. Whoever believes in me, as the Scripture has said, streams of living water will flow from within him." By this he meant the Spirit, whom those who believed in him were later to receive. Up to that time the Spirit had not been given, since Jesus had not yet been glorified.   ~ John 7:37-39

Fullness is actually commanded! Ephesians 5:18 admonishes us: "Be filled with the Holy Spirit!" This desire on God's part places it in our hearts as well. We long for a "Spirit-filled life." We realize our need for His fellowship and enabling for all phases of our lives — for our heart's hunger, for living our daily lives, for equipping us for special callings, for fruitfulness, for boldness, for the tests of suffering and sacrifice, and more.

Should we beg God like a miser? The Bible says He longs to give us His fullness! The believer's part is to fully accept His Lordship, then ask for His filling, and therefore receive the Spirit's fullness with thanksgiving. This is not a once-for-all process. We reaffirm His Lordship throughout our days, depend upon His indwelling Presence and power moment by moment, and thank Him for His gracious supply, to God's glory.

♥ *Have I accepted His Lordship, and affirmed His Spirit's presence, with thanksgiving?*

♥ *Do I habitually seek His filling?*

Prayer: *Scripture gives us the very prayer we need. We can earnestly pray Paul's prayer for the Ephesians for ourselves and for our fellowship of believers:*

> I pray that out of his glorious riches he may strengthen you with power through his Spirit in your inner being, so that Christ may dwell in your hearts through faith. And I pray that you, being rooted and established in love, may have power, together with all the saints, to grasp how wide and long and high and deep is the love of Christ, and to know this love that surpasses knowledge – that you may be filled to the measure of all the fullness of God. Now to him who is able to do immeasurably more than all we ask or imagine, according to his power that is at work within us, to him be glory in the church and in Christ Jesus throughout all generations, for ever and ever! Amen.
>
> ~ Ephesians 3:16-21

Ω

Hold on to the INDWELT KEY to being IN Christ:

To them God has chosen to make known among the
Gentiles the glorious riches of this mystery, which is
Christ in you, the hope of glory.

Colossians 1:27

Study 9

INHERITED

How can the gift of 'co-heirship' seen through Jewish eyes deepen appreciation for what is meant by the 'inheritance' of all believers?

(Drawn principally from the book of Hebrews and I Peter)

Introduction: As we move toward the close of the New Testament, the book of Hebrews provides a deeply Jewish view of the Messiah, and what it means to become His heirs. Fulfilling all of the Old Covenant types which God set into place in Moses' time, Jesus is seen as the ultimate and final Great High Priest of the Tabernacle. He made the sacrifice "once for all," finishing the work of redemption. His people look forward to sharing in the very inheritance of the Son of God.

Context: Studies 5, 6, 7, and 8 have focused upon God's marvelous promises for believers: the Gentiles "<u>ingrafted</u>" into the root; all believers given "<u>imputed</u>" righteousness through Christ's atonement; every believer "<u>included</u>" in all that was and is Christ's experience; and "<u>indwelt</u>" by the Spirit. These teachings are primarily found in Paul's letters to the fledgling churches in Gentile areas.

<u>**Heirship**</u> **is one more of God's inclusions for all believers,** even for Gentiles.

> *"There is neither Jew nor Greek, slave nor free, male nor female, for you are all one in Christ Jesus. If you belong to Christ, then you are Abraham's seed, and heirs according to the promise.* ~ Galatians 3:28-29

That was how Gentiles in Galatia were assured. Now let us go back to what was said to the Hebrew community. Looking through Jewish eyes at the tapestry of both covenants, we can glimpse a myriad of threads that weave a portrait of the Messiah that only Jewish understandings can provide.

Although written to explain New Covenant realities to Jewish believers while the Temple was still standing, Hebrews is a priceless gift to Gentile believers. It gives untaught non-Jews a short course in how the Old Covenant priesthood and sacrifices were conducted, how that system fell short of God's goal, and how the Messianic Son fulfilled and completed the work of redemption once for all, putting the whole sacrificial system to rest.

Consider the roles of Jewish-ness and Gentile-ness related to the mystery of God's ongoing purpose to draw the whole world to Himself. In that light, think about these questions:

Q. What do you think the Old Covenant community contributed?

Q. What do you think untaught Gentile converts contributed?

Q. Have you ever noticed evidences of a similar mystery in cross-cultural fellowship experiences shared in Christ today? An example?

Let's remember the "shadow and substance" concept taught in Hebrews, before looking at the book as a whole. It helps us see the two covenants' relationship in a fuller way. In Hebrews 8:5; 9:23 and 10:1, Old and New Covenant aspects are called "shadows" and "substance" (or "realities" in some translations). A shadow can sometimes be seen before the reality from which it is cast comes into view. It takes a tree to be, for its shadow to be seen. God's realities exist; therefore they cast shadows.

Like all the New Testament letters, Hebrews spoke to real life situations. Reading it, we can gather some issues on which their special community needed firm clarification. Imagine being an Israelite man or woman who has just discovered *Yeshua* to be the true Messiah and has just been baptized into Him. The Temple is still standing in the heart of Jerusalem. You are interacting in the atmosphere of the Temple and in community life with Israelites who have not believed in *Yeshua*, and some who firmly oppose your whole community. You are in growing relational tension.

Q. What do you think some of your doctrinal and practical struggles might be?

What needs does the letter to the Hebrews address? It was written to real men and women who were facing conflicting teachings. The opening chapters begin with a statement of the Son's superiority to angels of God and to Moses, Israel's great deliverer. Readers are called to remember Israel's unbelief in the wilderness years immediately following their miraculous deliverance from Egypt, and their unfaithfulness to the Sinai covenant with God. The writer challenges these 1st Century Christian readers not to fail to "enter into God's rest" like their forefathers failed. The letter explains the superiority of the Messiah's New Covenant.

A letter is meant to be read as a whole. The Spirit of God can speak much to us as we read Hebrews straight through. We can barely touch the tip of such a body of truth in these few pages, but there is deep reward for time invested in letting Hebrews permeate the soul. To accommodate for our brief study, however, below is a simple guide for exploring the "betterness" that Hebrews explains. *Chew on the meanings by trying to understand the "why" or "how" of Hebrews' "betters":*

First, the Son is <u>better</u> than all who preceded Him. (Hebrews 1)

> *In the past God spoke to our forefathers through the prophets, at many times and in various ways, but in these last days he has spoken to us by his Son, whom he appointed <u>heir of all things,</u> and through whom he made the universe. The Son is the radiance of God's glory and the exact representation of his being, sustaining all things by his powerful word.*
> ~ Hebrews 1:1-3a

This preamble tells us that the Son is appointed "heir of all things." It is from inclusion in Him that His people are said to "inherit" salvation (Hebrews 1:14). Hebrews 9:15 speaks of the "promised eternal inheritance" of believers. Remember that Israelites have long memories. They stretch back to God's promises to Abraham's family, and to Moses' community. The New Covenant carries those promises into their initial fulfillment phase.

Jesus is a <u>better High Priest</u> (Hebrews 4:14 – 5:10). *Why? How?*

His is a <u>better</u> Priesthood (Hebrews 5:4-10 and 7:1-28). See what ways the Levitical and Melchizedec (see Genesis 14:18-20) priesthoods are compared.

Write in your notes of comparison.

Levitical:	Melchizedek:

His is a <u>better covenant</u> (Hebrews 9 and 10). The first half of Hebrews 9 gives us a valuable short description of worship in the earthly Tabernacle. The rest of Hebrews 9 and chapter l0 compare elements of the worship that God set up in the wilderness comparing the old order with the new covenant brought in by the Son. We cannot appreciate the depth or the "betterness" of the covenant ratified by Christ's blood, if we are not versed in the old order and its animal sacrifices.

Jesus' ratification is made with <u>better blood</u> (Hebrews 9:11-14). <u>Blood</u> stands for <u>death</u> — the death penalty for sin.

Without the shedding of blood there is no forgiveness. ~ Hebrews 9:22b

Ever since the Fall, God has been working to bring life out of death, gain out of loss, moving from the Old to the New Covenant, the temporary to the eternal. Hebrews 9 shows us that a covenant must be ratified with blood. A legal will (the meaning of "testament") can only go into effect after the death of the testator. His death releases his inheritance as stated by his will. Scripture points out that even the Old Covenant in Moses' time was ratified by blood. In His mercy, God allowed the substitution of an animal's blood (death) for a man's death penalty. It took Christ's death to put the New Covenant — the new *testament* — into effect. This testament is the legal *will* that starts the process of releasing the inheritance to the inheritors. As put in Hebrews 9:15:

For this reason Christ is the mediator of a new covenant, that those who are called may receive the <u>promised eternal inheritance</u>—now that he has died as a ransom to set them free from the sins committed under the first covenant.

The New Covenant brings forth a <u>better result</u> (Hebrews 9:22-10:18). Not temporary and requiring endless repetition, Jesus' sacrifice was made once for all. This finished work of Christ brings forth <u>eternal</u> redemption, and releases an <u>eternal</u> inheritance. (See Hebrews 9:12-15.) The results are contrasted in Hebrews 9:22 to 10:28.

Write below the verse reference and some key words from the passages where these Old and New Covenant pairs are contrasted:

Earthly Tabernacle	True Tabernacle
Blood of animals	Blood of Christ
Repeated over and over	Once for all

THEREFORE...

After all the "since" truths that Hebrews has stated, the only reasonable response when reviewing what God has done is to respond with a "therefore...."!

"<u>Therefore</u> brothers, <u>since</u> we have confidence to enter the Most Holy Place by the blood of Jesus, by a new and living way opened for us through the curtain, that is, his body, and <u>since</u> we have a great priest over the house of God, <u>let us draw near to God with a sincere heart in full assurance of faith</u>.... ~ Hebrews 10:19-22a

"Let us…" is the Spirit's humble invitation to those He indwells. Tracing through Hebrews, "let us" can be found over and over. Listed are some of these gracious invitations. *Write down what each encourages the faithful to do:*

Hebrews 4:16

Hebrews 6:1

Hebrews 10:19-22

Hebrews 10:23

Hebrews 10:24

Hebrews 10:25

Hebrews 12:1-2

Hebrews 12:28-29

Hebrews 13:13

Hebrews 13:15

Look back at your notes above and try to see these passages through Jewish eyes. For instance, the first "let us" invitation was to approach the "throne of Grace." Realize that throne was the throne of Israel's God in the Holy of Holies in the Tabernacle, on the Mercy Seat! *Any other Jewish insights?*

The test of Lordship: The night before the cross, Jesus pleaded with His disciples, saying, "He that loves me keeps my commandments." The author of Hebrews speaks in that same vein as the book comes to a close. One behavior after another is put forth. Are they suggestions? No. We are called to love our Savior, the Lamb, but also to serve our King, the Lion of Judah. A King does not just "suggest." His wish should be our command. The blood of our Messiah King was shed...

"...to cleanse our consciences from acts that lead to death, so that we may serve the living God!"   ~ Hebrews 9:14b

How may we serve Him whom we love and to whom we owe our very lives? Sift through the end of Hebrews for a broad coverage of admonitions about the believers' life in the Spirit.

Make notes for yourself on the Scriptures below. Ponder the principles you find.

Hebrews 10:19-39 is focused on _____.

Hebrews 12:1-12 is focused on _____.

Hebrews 12:13-17 highlights what areas?

Hebrews 13:1-19 calls for what kinds of obedience?

Hebrews 11, "Faith's Hall of Fame," reminds us of the inheritance
our predecessors anticipated. Hebrews 11 displays an historical
overview of the readers' Jewish ancestors who kept the faith under
pressure, sometimes even to the point of martyrdom. The ancients
were commended for their *faith* — the certainty of what they did not
see. (Hebrews 11:1) "They looked for a city," the city of the living God
(Hebrews 12:22). The concluding thought of that wonderful summary
chapter is:

> *These were all commended for their faith, yet none of them received what*
> *had been promised. God had planned something better for us so that only*
> *together with us would they be made perfect.*   ~ Hebrews 11:39-40

Who is "us"? This means the 1st Century inheritors of the New
Covenant, the generation to which the letter to the Hebrews was
written. The next verse (12:1) is one of those "therefores," yet it still
applies to those of us who live farther down the line of promise, in
the Age of Grace.

> *Therefore, since we are surrounded by such a great cloud of witnesses, let us*
> *throw off every thing that hinders and the sin that so easily entangles, and*
> *let us run with perseverance the race marked out for us. Let us fix our eyes*
> *on Jesus, the author and perfecter of our faith, who for the joy set before him*
> *endured the cross, scorning its shame, and sat down at the right hand of the*
> *throne of God.*   ~ Hebrews 12:1-2

These early Christians living under pressure were no longer to rely
on animal sacrifices, but were to bring God something more inward
— "the sacrifice of praise" (Hebrews 13:15). They were freshly
aware of *Yeshua*'s fulfillment of the sacrificial system. We too may
live at variance with our dominant culture, so much so that we may
experience suffering and even martyrdom. May Jesus' joy and the
hope of our inheritance stay fresh within us to sustain us to persevere
and to endure!

**God delights to pour out His inheritance upon all who are "included
in Christ."** Surely this bounty should delight His inheritors, as well!

Peter's letter (contemporary with Hebrews) to suffering believers scattered by persecution calls attention to their *inheritance.* It is called their "blessed hope." In difficult times, assurance of a future inheritance keeps hope alive. *How fervently does I Peter 1:3-9 express how deeply this inheritance is appreciated, described, and awaited?*

There is a marvelous and secure invitation to "inheritors" at the end of Revelation. John is told to write Jesus' words:

> He said to me:"It is done. I am the Alpha and the Omega, the Beginning and the End.To him who is thirsty I will give to drink without cost from the spring of the water of life. He who overcomes will <u>inherit</u> all this, and I will be his God and he will be my son."   ~ Revelation 21:6-7

What does Jesus' *inheritor* **"look like"?** Your preceding "let us" list (page 96) gives a picture of what the believer's life and outlook can be, when filled with the Spirit. Thank God for whatever "agreement" you find in your spirit with His Spirit.

♥ *May my heart speak thankfulness for my filling, and praise for my being adopted into the blessings of Ephesians 1:3-6:*

Prayer: (a very Jewish conclusion)

> May the God of peace, who through the blood of the eternal covenant brought back from the dead our Lord Jesus, the great Shepherd of the sheep, equip you with everything good for doing his will, and may he work in us what is pleasing to him, through Jesus Christ, to whom be glory for ever and ever. Amen.

~ Hebrews 13:20-21

Ω

Hold on to the INHERITED KEY to life IN Christ:

For this reason Christ is the mediator of a new covenant, that those who are called may receive the promised eternal inheritance — now that he has died as a ransom to set them free from the sins committed under the first covenant.

Hebrews 9:15

Study 10

INFORMED

How has the Messiah prepared us for what to expect in the future?

(Drawn largely from I and II Peter and Revelation)

Introduction: A heart cry throughout the ages has been, "Will evil ever be judged? Will right ever triumph?" Although God has long restrained His hand of judgment, "the Day of the Lord" was foreseen throughout the Old Testament Scriptures. The prophets have warned us of the Day of God's wrath — from Isaiah's vision of the last days to Malachi's haunting question: "But who can endure the day of his coming? Who can stand when he appears?" (Malachi 3:2a) This line has been sung to crowds thousands of times over the last 300 years, in Handel's Messiah Oratorio. If listening, the world stands warned! The Spirit of God brings the New Testament to a close with an awesome revelation of the future from the glorified Jesus. The Apocalypse is placed after Peter's letters that deal with the suffering that believers should expect. The Revelation sees to it that we are not left hurtling into the future with no idea how all this will work out in the end. Humanity is informed, and being so, stands comforted and/or warned.

How has God informed us about what is called "the last days"?
This term is used in Deuteronomy 4:30, Hebrews 1:2, I Peter 1:20, etc. What are the future events He thinks the Body of Christ needs to be aware of as we pass through our pilgrimage toward the Heavenly City? (Bunyan's classic *Pilgrim's Progress* dramatized the Pilgrim's personal struggles on the way to that City.) Like a high-speed film, or multimedia, Revelation spreads a panorama of God's judgments before us coded in terms of "sevens." Then the last two chapters of Revelation give us a glimpse of the blessed hope that is to sustain the

faithful at "such a time as this." (*𝒥𝓵*'s Study 11 focuses on that final unfolding.)

Context: The book of Revelation is the capstone of prophecy, after centuries dotted with prophetic activity. Jesus is *The* Prophet who Moses said would finally come. While on earth, Jesus gave glimpses into the future through parables, spoke quite bluntly in "the Little Apocalypse" (Matthew 23-25), and then poured out the full Book of Revelation from heaven after His glorification at God's right hand.

Prophecy is a unique form of communication. As an important foundation for understanding it, consider how the Scriptures came about. Peter's writings explain the historical process of revelation that God gave to the prophets through the Holy Spirit's inspiration. *What does each of these passages tell us about prophecy?*

I Peter 1:10-12

II Peter 1:16-21

Placed just before the Revelation, Peter's letters focus especially upon the need for endurance and the assurance of our blessed hope during the testings of life in difficult times. Writing to believers scattered by persecution, Peter calls them to rejoice in their living hope:

Praise be to the God and Father of our Lord Jesus Christ! In his great mercy he has given us new birth into a living hope through the resurrection of Jesus Christ from the dead, into an inheritance that can never perish, spoil or fade — kept in heaven for you, who through faith are shielded by God's power until the coming of the salvation that is ready to be revealed in the last time.

~ I Peter 1:3-5

The passage above speaks about every believer's inheritance. *What does it say is the transaction that transfers our inheritance to us? How "protected" is this inheritance? How long will it last?*

I Peter 1:6-9 speaks of the mixture of trials and joy in believers' lives. *What is said about the normality of suffering, the end result of trials, and the odd accompaniment of "joy"?*

Keep your eye on the goal! The Letters generally move from factual truth to "therefore" applications. And so here:

> *Therefore, prepare your minds for action; be self-controlled; set your hope fully on the grace to be given you when Jesus Christ is revealed.*
>   ~ I Peter 1:13

We need always to keep our focus on the goal, our blessed hope — the end result after life's challenges.

"Be on guard!" (II Peter 3:17) In his second letter, Peter warns against false prophets and destructive teachings in the latter days, times when scoffers will taunt the faithful. *In II Peter 3:3-9, with what appeal to truth does Peter answer scoffers, and what reasons does he give for the Lord's "slowness" to keep the promise of His coming?*

We move now from the Letters to Revelation. Scholarship dates most of the Letters within the first few decades after the Resurrection. John's Revelation, however, is usually dated about AD 95, making it the final word of the New Covenant. John was the only Apostle left alive. The Temple in Jerusalem had been destroyed and the Israelites scattered abroad for about twenty-five years by the time the Spirit gave this revelation to John on the Isle of Patmos, on the coast of Asia, the location of the seven churches addressed at the beginning of the book.

Revelation is the book of ultimate fulfillment. The message of Revelation is both *forth*-telling and *fore*-telling, the two ministries of prophecy. It is the conclusion of the Biblical message, dealing with the climax of history. Jesus shines forth in the Revelation as the ultimate Priest, Prophet, and King — the three anointed offices so often shown in "types" in Old Covenant Times. Revelation opens with Jesus appearing as PRIEST in the midst of the seven golden lampstands. It proceeds with Jesus as PROPHET giving His message in vision form. It closes with Jesus identifying Himself as the soon-coming KING, the offspring of David.

Who is giving this revelation? Over and over Jesus the Christ identifies Himself. The One speaking to the churches then (and throughout history) is the One who came in the flesh (John 1:14), who identified Himself over and over as the "I AM," the One in whom Life is found (I John 5:12).

What "I AM" names does Jesus use to identify Himself in Revelation?

Revelation 1:17-18

Revelation 22:13

Revelation 22:16

Where did former prophetic disclosures come from? Little by little, God shared His plan with the prophets. Amos 3:7 tells us that,

> *"Surely the Sovereign LORD does nothing without revealing his plan to his servants the prophets."*

Revelation 10:7 says,

> *"But in the days when the seventh angel is about to sound his trumpet, the mystery of God will be accomplished, just as he announced to his servants the prophets."*

As the book of Revelation closes John says,

> *The angel said to me, "These words are trustworthy and true. The Lord, the God of the spirits of the prophets, sent his angel to show his servants the things that must soon take place."*   ~ Revelation 22:6

Jesus repeats His purpose in the last chapter,

> *"I, Jesus, have sent my angel to give you this testimony for the churches."*
> ~ Revelation 22:16a

Believers today are members of the universal church, and so the prophetic message to the seven churches applies to us as well. The prologue of Revelation, remember, promises <u>special blessing</u> to its true receivers:

> <u>*Blessed*</u> *is the one who reads the words of this prophecy, and <u>blessed</u> are those who hear it and take to heart what is written in it, because the time is near.*
> ~ Revelation 1:3

♥ *How much have I valued this special blessing?*

When and how should we read the Apocalypse? Often... and with the help of the Spirit of God! Revelation *informs* us. God does not want His people taken by surprise. He wants us to be prepared. He wants the world to be *warned* — through us. Only the Scriptures transmit this crucial message.

Studies 10 and 11 can only incompletely summarize Revelation's disclosures and perhaps stir up hunger for digesting this unique message that God promises to bless. It is a difficult book, a frightening message, poured out in a puzzling array of images beyond our understanding or even our imagination.

At last it concludes with a vision of hope (Biblical "hope" is *confident*) that awakens inexpressible joy. Believers are wise to read the entire book of Revelation at one sitting from time to time. Take it as a whole, setting puzzlements aside. At another time, its message can be explored and pondered section by section. Ask the Holy Spirit to interpret the Revelation's deep meaning to the heart, even if barely grasped by the mind.

♥ *How thirsty am I to understand Jesus' last message?*

♥ *What is the Spirit's main message to me as I read Revelation this time?*

A BRIEF SKETCH OF THE REVELATION SCROLL

Jesus, the High Priest (Revelation 1-3): The path of God's message to our hearts is revealed by the glorified Jesus: from God to Jesus, to an angel, to John, to the seven churches, to the communion of the saints (including us). In Revelation's opening chapter, the glorified Messiah stands among His people as their Priest. I Peter 4:17 in the KJV says that "judgment must begin at the house of God." Jesus speaks first to the seven churches — diagnosing their condition. His messages to the seven churches in Asia in chapters 2 and 3 show us His perception of His people's communities, hearts, and lives. He calls each to *repent* (except Philadelphia) and to *overcome*. He stands knocking at each heart's door, theirs then and ours now. (Revelation 3:20.) These last messages to the Church have warned the Body of Christ over the ages. Are the seven letters primarily the Messiah's intimate motivations to specific fellowships? Are they meant to prepare the universal Church for the temptations and warfare that believers will face throughout the ensuing centuries? Shall we think of them as reflecting a consecutive historical order? Any of these approaches will glean insights for our pilgrimage.

Jesus, the Lamb of God at the Throne (Revelation 4-5): The scene changes. Heaven opens. John is invited to behold an amazing revelation of what will soon be happening:

> *After this I looked, and there before me was a door standing open in heaven. And the voice I had first heard speaking to me like a trumpet said, "Come up here, and I will show you what must take place after this."*
>
> ~ Revelation 4:1

Immediately before John is God's throne in heaven. He who sits on the throne holds a scroll sealed with seven seals. An angel asks who is worthy to open the scroll, but no one in heaven or on earth is found worthy to open the scroll. John weeps. Then an elder says to John,

"Do not weep! See, the Lion of the tribe of Judah, the Root of David, has triumphed. He is able to open the scroll and its seven seals." Then I saw a Lamb, looking as if it had been slain, standing in the center of the throne....   ~ Revelation 5:5-6a

The worshippers fall down before the Lamb and sing a new song:

"You are worthy to take the scroll and to open its seals, because you were slain, and with your blood you purchased men for God from every tribe and language and people and nation. ...Worthy is the Lamb, who was slain.... To him who sits on the throne and to the Lamb, be praise and honor and glory and power, for ever and ever."
~ Revelation 5:9b, 12b, 13b

Chapters four and five are a precious gift to the Body of Christ. We learn that we are part of a great company of worshippers, and learn on whom God wants us to focus in worship, and why. Throughout the Apocalypse, other glimpses of heaven will be seen above the chaos happening on earth.

Jesus, Prophet of prophets (Revelation 4-19): Next, the future is unrolled before John's eyes. These chapters reveal God's final judgments and rewards. Down through the centuries God's people have been informed through John's eyes. He records what is humanly unimaginable — judgments on earth interspersed between worship in heaven (such as in chapter 7's glimpse of martyrs who have come out of the great tribulation, and other glimpses in chapters 11, 14, and 19). The Four Horsemen of the Apocalypse are loosed on earth — war, famine, plague and death. Indelible scenes cascade through time to a seven-beat drum roll, scenes flashing through billows of opened "seals" pouring out seven-fold judgments called "trumpets," "thunders," "plagues," "bowls" — woe upon woe. We glimpse catastrophic eschatological events in history — flash-backs and flash-forwards — Armageddon, the fall of Babylon, and the collapse of the whole world system.

Jesus, always the Redeemer (reminded in Revelation 14): The God who has "so loved the world" extends His mercy until the last hour. As Peter reminds those impatient for the finale,

He is patient with you, now wanting anyone to perish, but everyone to come to repentance. But the day of the Lord <u>will</u> come like a thief.
~ II Peter 3:9b-10a

In the midst of these horrific events, an angel gives one last opportunity to those on earth, to every nation, tribe, language and people:

Fear God and give him glory, because the hour of his judgment has come. Worship him who made the heavens, the earth, the sea and the springs of water. ~ Revelation 14:7

Over and over the world has been invited — not *commanded* to obey, but *invited* to come to Him. God has allowed each to make a personal choice. How long the Father has waited, yearning for humanity to choose Him, for our good, and for His joy! He longs for all to be gathered into His home envisioned in the final chapters of Revelation.

Jesus, warrior King, and judge (Revelation 19:11-20:15): At last, the Rider on the white horse appears, called "Faithful and True," and "the Word of God."

On his robe and thigh he has this name written: KING OF KINGS AND LORD OF LORDS. ~ Revelation 19:16

After a battle that destroys the forces of evil, Satan is bound for a thousand years. The "first resurrection" takes place. Yet once more Satan is released and deceives the nations again, and once more is defeated, and then cast into the lake of fire, the second death. The dead are judged by two books, and only those written in the Lamb's book of life will be delivered. With God's redemptive resolutions issued in, the joyous outworking of His ultimate will begins with the Father's invitation to a wedding, the Marriage Feast of the Lamb.

Jesus the Royal Bridegroom (Revelation 19:6-9; 21, 22): This is Jesus' parting message. What if we did not have the last two chapters of

Revelation? What a privilege to be given an authentic glimpse of the King of kings, His person, His work, His Bride, His city, His titles, and His imminent return. His last words in Revelation are:

"Yes, I am coming soon."

Those five words are each packed with significance, and summarize the message of Revelation. (Study 11 focuses on the joyous outworking of God's eternal purpose that was foretold in Ephesians 1:3-10.)

To conclude this brief overview of John's Apocalypse, we see that Scripture is full of responses to God's revelations and promises. "Therefore" or "so" marks the Biblical writers' pattern of worship or appeal. Peter puts a "so" to his readers, and therefore to us:

In keeping with his promise we are looking forward to a new heaven and a new earth, the home of righteousness. So then, dear friends, since you are looking forward to this, make every effort to be found spotless, blameless and at peace with him.   ~ II Peter 3:13-14

In those who love the Lord, there will be an eagerness to respond to His "therefore" admonitions. Here is a sample the Spirit gave through Peter:

Therefore prepare your minds for action, be self-controlled, set your hope fully on the grace to be given you when Jesus Christ is revealed.
~ I Peter 1:13

Peter warns us not to be surprised by suffering,

"But rejoice that you participate in the sufferings of Christ, so that you may be overjoyed when his glory is revealed.   ~ I Peter 4:13

In light of what the world faces inevitably, Jesus preceded His predictions with a call for His disciples' personal repentance and faithfulness. He asks His people to <u>endure</u> and to <u>overcome</u>. His indwelling Spirit is our resource for such a time as this. He has given us vital preparation in the Scriptures.

What assurances help you in the following passages?

On suffering: I Peter 4:12-19

On service: Revelation 1:5b-6

On "overcoming": Revelation 2:7, 17, 26; 3:5, 12, 21.
  (Each invitation is preceded by a call to repent.)

On endurance: Revelation 14:12

In the light of judgment coming upon the world, those who are
<u>informed</u> are therefore ambassadors, watchmen, warners, and
wooers, who bring a life-and-death message to their contemporaries.
The following Scriptures highlight the calling of "the informed."

What is the seriousness of "the <u>books</u>" that each person needs to
settle before their "departure time" and/or God's judgment day?
Revelation 13:8; 17:8; 20:12; 21:27

What do those IN Christ implore others to do? II Corinthians 5:16-21

What attitudes toward <u>suffering and questioning</u> does Peter
admonish? I Peter 3:8-17

What is said about perseverance during the last times? Jude 17- 25

In light of the joys promised to the people of God, Jesus closes Revelation with glimpses of a marvelous completion. The Bridegroom trusts the Bride to "love His appearing." (Study 11 will focus on those joyous realities.)

♥ *In Revelation 1:3, Jesus promises blessings to those who read and hear His prophecy and take it to heart. After reading Jesus' letters to His own, and seeing a panorama of the end times, what are some of my heart responses?*

Prayer: *Lord, purify my heart. As I take my place within the royal priesthood of your Kingdom, may I bring you the sacrifice of praise, and may your Spirit assist me to sing with the saints that new song of Revelation 5:9-10, 13b:*

> You are worthy to take the scroll and to open its seals, because you were slain, and with your blood you purchased men for God from every tribe and language and people and nation. You have made them to be a kingdom and priests to serve our God, and they will reign on the earth. ... To him who sits on the throne and to the Lamb be praise and honor and glory and power, for ever and ever! Amen.

Ω

Hold on to the INFORMED KEY to life IN Christ:

When I saw him, I fell at his feet as though dead. Then he placed his right hand on me and said: "Do not be afraid. I am the First and the Last. I am the Living One; I was dead, and behold I am alive for ever and ever! And I hold the keys of death and Hades. Write, therefore, what you have seen, what is now and what will take place later."

Revelation 1:17-19

Study II

INVITED

What is "the end of the story" — the believers' "blessed hope"?

(Drawn principally from the close of Revelation and related Scriptures)

Introduction: Scripture closes with Jesus being the focus of our blessed hope, the Alpha and Omega — the First and Last. He is calling us to Himself! And His Bride is calling for Him to come quickly! The roles of the Messiah foreshadowed in the Old Testament are all fulfilled. The Messiah has been incarnated and become the Second Adam, has paid the price for our redemption. He has been vindicated by the Father through His resurrection. He has been glorified and has poured out His Spirit on all who are IN Christ. His incarnational presence has continued in His people, as they are <u>imputed</u> with His righteousness, <u>ingrafted</u> into the root, <u>included</u> in all that is Christ's, <u>indwelt</u> by the Spirit of God, <u>inherited</u> in union with the Heir, and <u>informed</u> of the future. Now we come to the glorious future into which we are <u>invited</u>. In Revelation, those gathered into that great company that constitute His Bride are invited to the Wedding Banquet, and shown the radiance of the Bride in the Groom's eyes as she takes her place on the throne. The Lamb is the very light of the New Heaven and New Earth. Those within the Bride are enraptured, amazed, longing, crying out, "Come, Lord Jesus!"

Context: This nearly final *IN* study brings us to the completed restoration toward which history has been moving. Study 10 introduced the book of Revelation and moved from the Messiah's opening letters to His churches, on into John's vision of "what will soon come to pass." Worship in heaven and judgment on earth swirl before us in the Apocalypse. Are the seven-fold judgments chronological, or a broad drama applicable throughout history up to the final Day of God? Whichever or both, in the end the goal of God is realized through the Son, by the Holy Spirit. All is fulfilled, and the joy of a New Heaven and New Earth breaks through.

Let us look back at Old Testament predecessors of the final revelation. We have traced the Messiah throughout the Scriptures in the companion studies *ALL* and *IN*, with an emphasis on the Bible's Jewish context. God sent His message into the world through His covenant people Israel, and through His Son, who was also the son of Adam, son of Abraham, and son of David. The Spirit of God communicated the reality of who the Son is through analogies humans can understand and remember. Old Covenant roles of the "anointed ones" were like shadow outlines of the reality that appeared to us in the Incarnation. The Word became flesh. (John 1:14a) In summary, Jesus of Nazareth was and is the ultimate SEED, SON, LAMB, PRIEST, HOST, PROPHET, and KING.

The agreement of the Scriptures covers centuries. Having looked through Jewish eyes in the preceding studies, we have been alerted to these roles, and behold, they appear again throughout the book of Revelation. The vision was given to a Jewish Apostle who is communicating with Jewish people who will then interpret the Gospel to Gentile believers. These messianic roles are actual facets of the Lord Jesus Christ's person, not imagined characters in a play.

A way to approach a search through the Scriptures: Picture a researcher using a "magnet" that is attracted to the various "metals" of the Messiah's seven roles. We can draw the magnet through the Bible to pick up "filings" that are attracted. The results can be thrilling. Try passages in Revelation.

On the following chart, draw a line across to connect each reference in Revelation on the left to a matching role that is listed on the right:

Revelation 12:13-17	KING
Revelation 2:18	PROPHET
Revelation 5:6; 22:1-3	HOST
Revelation 1:12-14	PRIEST
Revelation 19:7	LAMB
Revelation 19:10b; 22:6-7	SON
Revelation 19:16	SEED

How marvelous to see how the Old and New Testaments weave a tapestry with these multicolored interwoven threads. The Messiah is the pattern that emerges!

The Apocalypse needs bi-cultural (native and Jewish) reading. Gentile Bible readers without Jewish understandings miss much of the meaning and implicated fullness of the Book of Revelation. The vision is deeply invested with meanings from the culture of the Old Testament with its "shadows" — such as the symbolism of the Tabernacle and Feasts. We find there are references to the "seven" code word, the High Priest's vestments, the menorah lights, the tree of life, manna, Jezebel, the temple, Jerusalem, the throne, scrolls, seals, the Lion of the tribe of Judah, the Lamb that was slain, the Root of David, the twelve tribes, white robes, palm branches, the mercy seat, censers, altars, trumpets, plagues, olive trees, lamp stands, beasts, horns, Sodom, Egypt, Babylon, and more. Each term includes implied meanings that may be filled in by their Old Testament predecessors. There are New Testament predecessors as well, and it is their fulfillment in the last two chapters of Revelation that we are focusing upon in Study 11. The New Testament repeatedly lifts up the believers' crowning hope — "His appearing"! A crown of righteousness is rewarded to those who "have loved His appearing"! (II Timothy 4:8) *Love* is the language of romance, the language between a bride and groom.

Jewish marriage customs throw light on the closing chapters of Revelation. Jesus in John 14:1-4 told His disciples that He was going to "prepare a place" for them. He had also told marriage-related parables (like the king's invitation to his son's wedding banquet, and the ten virgins at midnight, in Matthew 22 and 25). He was speaking to Jews who understood their context. A Jewish suitor was as good as married to his betrothed, but had to go to add rooms to his father's house before the marriage could be consummated. Only the father could say when the marriage could be held. (Consider the "unknown hour" Jesus spoke of in Matthew 24:36, in this light.) Both bride and groom waited for that signal. Often the groomsmen came for the bride at night, to take her to the home the groom had prepared. Invited guests were those of one's own family or community, but in Jesus' parable, most rejected the invitation and then it went out to the highways and byways, even to Gentiles (Matthew 22:1-10).

The imminence of the Lord's return is the focus of "our blessed hope"! His return for His bride has been in the Bridegroom's heart even as He spoke of it mysteriously on earth. That return is the crowning fact with which the Apostles comforted their people. It would be a time of vindication, of fulfillment, of restoration, of reward, of consummation. This culmination is beginning to happen at the end of Revelation. In that light, the Bride's final cry in the Scriptures is, "Come, Lord Jesus!"

Fill your heart with these precious promises to the Bride — all IN Christ:

Matthew 16:24-27

John 5:24-27

John 14:1-3

I Corinthians 15:20-26

I Corinthians 15:50-57

Philippians 2:5-11

Believers await the trumpet sound on tiptoe! So keenly did early Christians expect the Lord's return that they grieved when someone died before this rapturous expectation was fulfilled. Paul comforts them with a reminder of the promise to all believers, both those who had died and those still waiting. Each line is full of meaning:

For the Lord himself will come down from heaven, with a loud command, with the voice of the archangel and with the trumpet call of God, and the dead in Christ will rise first. After that, we who are still alive and are left will be caught up together with them in the clouds to meet the Lord in the air. And so we will be with the Lord forever. Therefore encourage each other with these words.   ~ I Thessalonians 4:16-18

"The Rapture" (caught up) is the English term that was coined for our Lord's coming for the Church, His Bride. Just when the wedding and the coming will occur, only the Father knows. Biblical interpretations differ on whether the Bridegroom's arrival to take His Bride will happen before, during, or after the Tribulation. They differ on whether there will be a preliminary catching up of believers into the clouds, or combined with our Lord's Second Coming to earth. The certainty is that our Lord has promised to return. In the Father's timing, IT WILL HAPPEN.

Finally, we see the promise coming to fruition at the end of Time and the beginning of Eternity. First, the Wedding is announced:

> *Let us rejoice and be glad and give him glory! For the wedding of the Lamb has come, and his bride has made herself ready.... Then the angel said to me, "Write: Blessed are those who are invited to the wedding supper of the Lamb! And he added, "These are the true words of God."*
>
> Revelation 19:7, 9

Who is invited, and who is the Bride? (See Matthew 22:1-8 for clues.)

♥ *Do you expect to be there?*

Then Eternity opens before us in Revelation 21 and 22. Revelation brings us full circle, from the blighted garden to the eternal one. God has been bringing His rescue to pass ever since God graciously banished our fallen parents from the tree of Life that would keep them living forever in their fallen state. By His grace, those who accept His rescue are restored to the fullness of God's garden that is watered by a river flowing from the throne of God and of the Lamb. He has accomplished His desire, to dwell with us!

And I heard a loud voice from the throne saying, "Now the dwelling of God is with men, and he will live with them ... and be their God. He will wipe every tear from their eyes. There will be no more death or mourning or crying or pain, for the old order of things has passed away."

~ Revelation 21:3-4

Take a deep breath, and behold! It is good to try to read right through Revelation 21 and 22 at one sitting. Try to see it through new eyes and hear it like someone who has never heard the Biblical message before.

With what is God gifting His inheritors? What is no longer needed or present? What is all new?

Read those two last chapters again, as a bride awaiting the return of her lover. Ask the Spirit of God to speak to you anew through it. *What most engages your mind or touches your heart in these two chapters?*

Man says "seeing is believing." God says "believing is seeing." If we are believing, we are privileged to *see* and *hear* what is happening in heaven through the vision John was given. Worship can take on a whole new reality as it is revealed in the book of Revelation. We see more fully who our Lord IS, how His Father has enthroned Him, and hear the praise of God's angels and the saints who have gone before us.

♥ **Being the Bride:** *Ask the Spirit of God to quicken your heart to join in these scenes of worship listed below. You may be a participant in them, by the time all is finished:*

Revelation 5:6-14

Revelation 7:9-17

"Come" is the most often repeated *invitation* word in Revelation. Tracing through Revelation, these are a few of those "comes":

➤ *Here I am! I stand at the door and knock. If anyone hears my voice and opens the door, I will come in and eat with him, and he with me....*

➤ *Come up here and I will show you what must take place after this....*

➤ *For the wedding of the Lamb has come....*

➤ *Come, and I will show you the bride, the wife of the Lamb....*

➤ *Whoever is thirsty, let him come, and whoever wishes, let him take the free gift of the water of life.*

➤ *Yes, I am coming soon.*

The two shall be one. God has come to us in Creation, and His Son in Redemption, and His Spirit in His indwelling. The lover waits to be received, and to hear the responsive "Yes, yes come, Lord Jesus!"

♥ *My heart, be enthralled with the Bridegroom, realize His love and patient expectancy, be deeply joyous "in" Him!*

Prayer: *The Bride being prepared to come into her Groom's glorious presence can be encouraged by the benediction of Jude:*

> To him who is able to keep you from falling and to present you before his glorious presence without fault and with great joy — to the only God our Savior be glory, majesty, power and authority, through Jesus Christ our Lord, before all ages, now and forevermore. Amen.

~ Jude 24-25

Ω

Hold on to the INVITED KEY to life IN Christ:

Then the angel said to me, "Write: blessed are those who are invited to the wedding supper of the Lamb!" And he added, "These are the true words of God."

Revelation 19:9

Study 12

"INVERTED"

What traditions have distorted the Biblical reality of being IN Christ?

(Drawn largely from history compared with Biblical truth)

Introduction: We have come to the close of *IN*'s preceding chapters that have been focused on God's various gifts of "in-ness" to the believer born of the Spirit. We have delved into the Scriptures, appreciating our Lord's marvelous revelations about the *integration* of the Old and New Testaments, and our Lord's *Incarnation* reported in the Gospels. According to the book of Acts, ever since the age of the Spirit was *inaugurated*, true believers are *ingrafted* into Israel, as Romans 11 teaches. The Letters go on to reveal that believers' acceptance with God is on the basis of an *imputed* righteousness; that we are *included* in Christ; we are *indwelt* by the Spirit; and we look forward to the riches which the regenerate have *inherited*. In the book of Revelation we are *informed* about the future and that the redeemed are *invited* to the Wedding Banquet inaugurating the new age. How absolutely marvelous!

Without God's having revealed these truths to us, however, we would be oblivious of them. We who have the Scriptures may carelessly take them for granted, but only God could have conferred such riches upon us, and only He could have revealed them.

♥ *Please go to the close of this book to the page of IN's "key verses" representing these amazing revelations.*

How important are they to your own spiritual life?
Record some personal responses here:

This final Study 12 focuses on how these "INs" of Scripture were "inverted" — largely "turned on their heads" — during the long "wilderness wanderings" of Christendom. Webster defines "inversion" as "being reversed, or turned inside out." How could this have happened? Were these basic Scriptural truths not understood? Forgotten? How did substitutions take over? What caused them to be replaced with human inventions?

We today are blessed to be Word-of-God-informed! Having just recorded some actualities you have experienced in your own personal life, now imagine NOT knowing any of these things, because of NOT having the very words of God. Suppose you had never had in your hands the record of His promises. This was the condition of Christian communities in many countries throughout the Middle Ages. Only priests were allowed to handle the Word of God, not the congregation's common people. The Scriptures were often restricted to holy languages and not allowed in a vernacular.

Considering how far afield history shows Christendom to have wandered, it seems unlikely that the leadership based their teachings on the plain meanings of the Scriptures. Furthermore, without the enlightenment of the Spirit, these marvelous but mysterious facts about the "reborn" (John 3:7, I Peter 1:3) could not have been grasped, let alone taught. Christian history reveals centuries of the "remnant's"

(Romans 11:5) struggles to recapture Scriptural truth. As warned by *Austin's Topical History of Christianity*, "Unless one knows where he has come from, he cannot understand where he is, nor foresee where he is going."

Frank admission: This Study 12, by trying to analyze a broad swath of history, attempts more than *𝓜*'s space or scholarship allows. The author's purpose is to raise interest in the serious problems that Christendom's legacy presents us with yet today. Let's consider what it would be like to have little familiarity with the Biblical wealth *𝓜*'s preceding chapters have explored. We may uncover unBiblical misinterpretations and manipulations that still cripple our actual appropriation of God's overflowing gifts to the "reborn." *Reviewing even a couple of books that undergird Study 12's assertions would be time well spent for the reader motivated to investigate these vital matters further. Here are two:*

Fox's Book of Martyrs (1563, updated repeatedly over the centuries, including in 1926), originally by John Foxe, is the venerable classic that recorded religious persecution. Of Foxe's book, Google states: "After the Bible itself, no book so profoundly influenced early Protestant sentiment." It recounts the lives and deaths of the faithful, starting with Jesus, Stephen, the Disciples, Nero's victims, early church fathers like Ignatius and Polycarp, and through the years, men like Ridley, Latimer, Wycliffe, Huss, and Tyndale, along with named and unnamed martyrs who were burned at the stake, drowned, and otherwise silenced. Following in the train of the heroes of Hebrews 11, these are those "of whom the world was not worthy." We have them to thank for the access to the Word and the freedom of religion that we enjoy today, although most of us are oblivious to the price they paid for their availability.

The Reformers and Their Stepchildren (1964, reprinted repeatedly, including in 2004) by Leonard Verduin is a more recently collected source. Verduin recounts lives of dissenters over the centuries who pled for Scripture to be made available to the common man and who cried for reforms in Christendom long before the Reformation, and some thereafter. Hounded as "heretics," they suffered greatly and sometimes paid with their lives. Verduin's book presents hundreds of case studies in chapters based on derogatory names with which they were branded and punished: "staff-carriers" (not sword carriers); "heretics" (anti-Church views); "cleansed" (characterized by holy living); "unauthorized" (by the State Church) "sacramentarians" (opposing extra-Biblical interpretations of the Mass); "communists" (sharing goods); "agitators" (against false doctrines); "Anabaptists" (re-baptizing an adult on profession of faith, although christened as an infant), "clandestine gatherers" (meeting secretly); etc.

♥ *Please ask yourself how these "inversions" of Biblical truths may have happened. Jot down reasons that come to your mind either from history, or from knowing human nature.*

Let's review what was largely lost for centuries. Through the Scriptures, the Holy Spirit gave the believing community mysterious but precious "in" revelations about the amazing actualities shared by all within the true Body of Christ. The pouring out of the Spirit (Acts 2) to replace and glorify the Incarnate Son on earth came fifty days after His Cross and Resurrection. At the Church's birth, multiple languages fell from the Spirit upon people from many nations. The new community found itself to be not just Jewish, not even *inter*national, but *supra*national! The exalted Messiah King was gathering a Kingdom not of this world and entered voluntarily by accepting His Lordship. The Kingdom of God does not compete or fight to take over earthly kingdoms, yet it profoundly influences them all.

The believing "remnant" of Christ-ones found themselves to be living *alongside* their pagan secular citizens, or, after Rome's Constantine, *within* a "Christen*dom*-ized" state. Emperor Constantine's proclamation that the Roman Empire was to be "Christian" seemed at first to be helpful to previously persecuted believers. But new problems arose. Jews were all the more persecuted. Furthermore, as a result of the merging of church and state from the time of Constantine onward (330s AD), the purity of the earlier ecclesia began to be compromised. Access to the Word was suppressed among common people and all kinds of manipulative changes emerged.

The influence of Augustine (354-430) on Church doctrine was stabilizing and profound. Yet unscriptural practices were undergirded by his *allegorical* (not plain, literal) *interpretation* of Scripture. What we now call "Replacement Theology" taught the Church's supersession over Israel, saying the Church had "replaced" Israel. It dismissed the Hebrew Root of the faith, and redefined the Church as having begun with Abraham, not Pentecost. Note that the traditions of Abraham and Israel were pre-Cross, pre-Pentecost, pre-New Testament revelation. Instead of the "new wine" concepts of the New Covenant (Jesus' explanation in Luke 5:36-38), the earlier "old wine" modes became employed in the service of Christendom's power structures. The old wine was wonderful as predictive shadows to be kept "exactly according to the pattern" (Exodus 25:9) so as to eventually be fulfilled "exactly," but the shadows were not meant to be replaced by religiously reworked "traditions."

What kind of substitutions were created? Christening infants (parallel to Jewish circumcision) was substituted for believer baptism. New doctrines about the Mass (employing symbolism and authority akin to Temple practices) were substituted for simple communion and primary focus on the Word. Birth into a realm and even forced "conversions" were substituted for voluntary entrance into the believing community. A formal hierarchical priesthood (similar to Old Testament times) replaced the New Covenant's "priesthood of the believers." Church *traditions* became considered as authoritative as Scripture. We remember that Jesus called the Pharisees and teachers of the law to account, saying, "you nullify the word of God for the sake of your traditions" (Matthew 15:6b). In the midst of these traditions, the presence and power of the Holy Spirit sent to earth for the Age of Grace seemed to be largely ignored.

False principles prevailed. Christendom throughout the Middle Ages was expected to spread by natural birth into a "Christian" king's realm or by warfare at the point of the ruler's sword. Dissenters argued that Biblical salvation came through the Word of God (Romans 10:17, I Peter 1:23). But to teach that salvation was a gift to be freely chosen, activated by rebirth into the *supra*national Kingdom of God, was deemed "heretical."

We do well to re-examine the principles and doctrines for which the believing remnant contended, suffered, and often were martyred. Dr. J.S. Whale of Oxford and Cambridge put it this way: "Dissent, not only from the centralized absolutism of Rome, but also from the State establishments of Protestantism in the Old World is an historic fact of enduring significance. To account for the tradition of liberty in the 'free world' of today without reference to dissent would be to read modern history with one eye shut."

♥ *Consider your own background. How did your early faith community conceive of entrance into Christ's Kingdom? How did your faith community teach the key to acceptance before God?*

We have basked in these "*IN*" studies in the overwhelming spiritual inheritance of believers, both in time and in eternity. Had we not been given the revelation and assurance of God's Word, our lives would be incredibly different. That the awareness of these riches could have been omitted and "inverted" for centuries is an appalling fact. Yet we can realize how this could have happened because we understand something of human nature and the cleverness of the Enemy. Lest we fall into similar traps in our own generation, we need to discern error and "inversions" instigated by Satan's on-going warfare against the people of God in our present times.

***

Let's look now at evidence of manipulations in terms of Biblical "IN's" being inverted. *Please jot down the main point of each reference in the* "non" *categories below:*

Non-Inaugurated: Early in Christian history, the Church was declared to have begun with Abraham, not created at Pentecost. Everything from Abraham on was considered to be the inheritance of the Church, "replacing" Israel. While the Trinity became an honored doctrine, the actual work of the Holy Spirit in the life of a believer seemed overlooked.

How crucial and significantly timed was God's gift of the Holy Spirit?

John 7:39

John 14:16-17

Acts 1:8

Acts 2:32-33

I Corinthians 2:14

Colossians 1:26-27

Ephesians 1:13-14

Non-Ingrafted: As Gentiles growingly outnumbered Jewish adherents, the original decisions of the Jerusalem Council established in Acts 15 seemed forgotten. Gentile branches <u>did</u> persistently "boast over the root" into which they were grafted, as warned against in Romans 11:17-18. Israel became ostracized, "replaced," set aside. The Jewish roots of the Church were dismissed and Hebraic forms were cleansed out. Even Jews were forbidden to keep their Sabbaths and Biblical Feasts. The solar replaced the Biblical lunar calendar. New feasts were instituted, some tied to the Incarnation, but many memorializing outstanding Christians who the Church eventually canonized as "saints." Considering Rome's destruction of Jerusalem in 70 AD and the scattering of the Jewish people, we can understand how easily this "replacement" assumption could have conveniently developed, if not checked by the clear teachings of Scripture.

What were Biblical teachings about Jew/Gentile relationships?

Acts 15:1-2, 13-21

Romans 10:12-13

Romans 11:13-24

Ephesians 2:14-16

How sovereignly chosen and perpetually loved is Israel?

Deuteronomy 4:37-38

Jeremiah 31:3

Luke 1:32-33

Romans 9:4-5

Romans 11:28-29

Revelation 7:3-8; 21:12

Non-Imputed: "Righteousness" must have become a touchy subject, especially in a Christendom thought to consist of all physically born into a certain realm. If righteousness was not understood to be "imputed" as a gift to the reborn, then other efforts for the mixed multitude to attain righteousness had to be invented. Examples: re-interpretations related to the Mass, the confessional, indulgences, purgatory, etc. These were issues which the Reformation in the 1500's eventually had to address and which Rome's ensuing Counter-Reformation faced, as well.

How is striving by one's own works to accomplish a "righteous" status in God's sight unBiblical?

Romans 9:31-32

Romans 10:1-4

Galatians 2:21

Titus 3:4-7

Non-Included: The truth that being reborn "in Christ" and thus included in all Christ's inheritance was replaced by false assumptions of being physically born and christened into an ecclesiastical and political realm which claimed to have inherited all of disenfranchised Israel's blessings. Furthermore, Christendom assumed the right to force people into its realms by various forms of coercion including the sword. "Convert, be exiled, or die" were often the choices given to Jews, dissenters, and the conquered.

What warnings has Scripture given about the nature of God's Kingdom, and how it is entered?

Matthew 7:14

John 18:36-37

Acts 2:38-41

Acts 3:17-20

Romans 10:9-13

Related to this issue, we need to be aware that references to "the chosen, the called, the elect" need to be kept in balance as we try to understand the paradox of the free will of man and the sovereignty of God.

Non-Indwelt: The Biblically-taught entrance of the Holy Spirit related to an act of the believer's repentance and faith was replaced by a vague sense of spirituality dependent upon being in right standing with the Church through christening, celebration of the Mass, the confessional, etc.

Consider these principles:

John 15:5

I Corinthians 1:18

I Corinthians 2:12-14

Is it reasonable to expect unconverted, unregenerate people to actually have received the Spirit's resources for holy living?

Non-Inherited: The precious inheritance of all true believers was taught in Scriptures such as I Peter 1:1, 3-7. But without the Bible, the common people could hardly have been made aware of their unconditional inheritance. "Conditional" benefits under priestly control and based on certain criteria set up by the Church were substituted, such as receiving merit through rituals, indulgences, and other means.

According to Scripture, who make up the "priesthood of believers" since the Cross, Resurrection, and Pentecost's provision of the Holy Spirit?

Ephesians 2:19-22

I Peter 2:5, 9

Revelation 20:6

Non-Informed: Knowledge of Biblical eschatology was lacking or interpreted allegorically. Art work depicting prophetic scenarios and scenes of judgment were used as substitutes. Without God's Word in their hands, how could the common people be alerted to Biblical warnings and encouragements about the consummation of God's eternal plan?

How important for every believer were Jesus' and the Apostles' warnings about the future?

Matthew 7:14

Matthew 24:36-42

Matthew 25:1-13

Luke 21:20-28 (Romans 11:25)

II Peter 3:3-13

Revelation 3:14-22

Non-Invited: Without Revelation's concluding chapters, a believer was denied the expectancy of God's assurances, the joy of anticipation, and clarity about who will enjoy life in His Kingdom. *For examples:*

Matthew 20:16

Luke 14:15-24

Revelation 19:7-9

Revelation 21:27

Where but in Scripture could these authentic revelations be found?!

Beloved reader, God's truths are either truly true or not true at all, not even worth discussing — which is the viewpoint of sophisticated modern man. Believers must realize that Truth can't be tampered with, forgotten, replaced, or inverted, without tremendous damage to those who seek God, and to the rest of humanity. The heart-cries of the prophets like Jeremiah and Hosea, and Jesus' lament over Jerusalem (Matthew 23:37-39) uttered God's anguish over these matters. We hear God's heart in Paul's groaning over Israel's lostness in Romans 9:2, "I have great sorrow and unceasing anguish in my heart."

***

We ask, "How could these destructive INVERSIONS have happened?" Scripture gives us the basic answer to this question. It is actually no mystery, but is a reality we face, a reality unacknowledged by many today.

Who is shown to be at war with God and humanity, constantly pursuing God's beloved? Here are a few informative glimpses:

Genesis 3:1-4, 14-15

Job 1:6-12; 2:1-6

Matthew 4:1-11

John 8:44

Ephesians 6:10-11

Revelation 12:13-17

Satan has cleverly and perpetually manipulated people to distrust God ever since the Fall. He encourages misuse of the Scriptures and obstructs its access. Evil men also "suppress the truth," as Romans 1:18 reminds us. In addition, God's Enemy has marshalled Adamic man's will-to-power in his own crafty service. How else could the two communities who Biblically were to be "one new man" (Ephesians 2:15) have turned so vehemently against each other? How else could Jews have been pursued, vilified, and almost exterminated over and over again — by the Pharaoh in Moses' time, Haman in Esther's time; Rome in the lst Century, the Inquisition and Pogroms throughout the Middle Ages; and Hitler in contemporary memory? Neo-Nazism, Anti-Semitism, and militant Islam continue in the Enemy's service today. Embarrassingly and tragically, Christendom has been implicated repeatedly.

We wonder, "Why has the world languished so long, unreached?" History shows us that when the Church became identical with society, the impetus to encourage voluntary response to the Gospel was overlooked. Many had theological instruction, but were not aware of the need for intentional appropriation of a personal relationship with the Lord Jesus. And it would be a couple centuries after the Reformation before the Protestant churches began to reach out to the need of the world as a whole through modern missions.

Today believers are challenged to admit and confess the Church's corporate sins, especially against Israel. Paul's invaluable teaching in Romans 11 clarified our roles. God through the Jews gave the Scriptures and the Messiah to the Gentiles. The Gentiles were to bring the Messiah to the Jews — to make them "jealous" (Romans 11:11 RSV). Yet instead, the Gentiles have helped make them hardened. It appears that Israel and the Church both have promises that God is still waiting to fulfill.

Considering our risen Lord's commission (Matthew 28:19-20) to the Church, God may be allowing His people to have a part in His timing. He may be waiting for us to reach the "full number of Gentiles." He may be waiting for "one new man" to blossom into reality, so that the world may believe.

Consider these Scriptures:

Matthew 24:14

Romans 11:25-27

Romans 11:28-32

Ephesians 2:14-22

How can we today be alert to recognize Satan's deceptions that continue to disable the Church? Well, certain mainstays of manipulation can be seen in Christianity's checkered history since the Incarnation. Imagine the panoramic overview of the ages by the analogy of an accordion pulled out to its widest extension. When the instrument is pressed together to force out sound, we see its vertical spines lined up. When we press in 2000 years of AD history together, we see the skeletal pillars that the Deceiver has so cleverly used to confuse and confound the Chosen People and the Church in his warfare against humanity's faith in the God the Enemy so hates. The basic "accordion spines" show up clearly: Silence the Word, manipulate the sacraments, coerce by the sword, "humor" concepts of "sin" and "rebirth," stifle freedom of choice, exploit humanity's proud independent spirit, silence dissent, substitute organizational modes for the work of Spirit...and more.

Let us remember that the Enemy is still at war with all of God's people, everywhere, all the time. He devises new ways to entice every generation with old deceptions. Our Lord calls us to be awake to the *inversions* of our own times! Some of them are inherited from the legacy of history, and some are devised by the Enemy for this particular age.

What are we warned to learn from Israel's history?

I Corinthians 10:1-12

♥ *Where have you sensed similar manipulations in your own experience? Using our "in" categories, here are issues to consider:*

Inaugurated: Do our fellowships seem to intentionally depend upon the Holy Spirit, or are we pretty dependent on organization? *My observation:*

Ingrafted: Are the grafted-in branches, even my own, "boasting against the root"? Are congregations being taught to assume that Israel has been "superseded" and "replaced"? *My experience:*

Imputed: Do we sense attitudes assuming that righteousness before God can be gained through our own good works? *Examples:*

Included: Are we clear, and concerned, about who the Bible says are "included" in all the benefits of Christ's saving work? How many nominal or even practicing Christians and Messianic Jews are missing the accomplished redemption and spiritual resources of being "in Christ"? *My concern:*

Inherited: Are we or our congregation more invested in our earthly than our heavenly inheritance? Do we deeply appreciate the true believers' imperishable inheritance (I Peter 1:4)? *My conclusion:*

Informed: Are we aware of and serious about meeting the One everyone must meet, either as Savior or Judge? Are we prepared and eager for our Lord's return? *My heart:*

Invited: How earnestly are those considering themselves to be within the Bride waiting for the Wedding Supper of the Lamb? Are today's congregations demonstrably looking forward to God's climactic fulfillment with joyful anticipation? *My observation:*

***

The 500ᵗʰ anniversary of the Reformation has arrived. For the Reformation's return to the Scriptures and proclamation of justification by faith alone, we can be deeply thankful. However, Christendom was not fully "reformed" in the 1500's. Some Biblical foundations have only been restored in the last few centuries. Vestiges of our unBiblical legacy still influence the theology and practice of most denominations, even today. "Replacement Theology" is one un-reformed legacy that continues. The anti-Semitism of Church fathers, including Luther, is an example of human fallibility even in those history most admires. It bore bitter fruit in the Holocaust, and threatens Jews still, today. On the other hand, growing numbers of Jewish believers in Jesus as the Messiah — the "budding of the olive tree" — may be a harbinger of the close of "the times of the Gentiles" (Luke 21:24, Romans 11:25) and at last, "His appearing" (Titus 2:13)!

♥ *What am I personally convicted about doing, changing, exploring, praying about, enjoying in light of these "in"-related issues and their consequences?*

PRAYER:

> Oh dear Father, how earnestly my heart needs to believe Your truth, and therefore to live in the fullness of the Spirit who is indwelling all who are truly reborn into Your family! Thank You for my Savior's righteousness that You mercifully impute to me. May I appropriate more and more of Your "in-ness" — in dwelling me, ingrafting me, including me, and informing me. Oh that I might grasp the height and depth of Your love, be encouraged and refreshed in my spirit, and bask in Your Son's inheritance shared with Your whole family.

Turn my heart to the lost world You so love, so that You may be known, loved, worshipped, and glorified throughout the world You created. In the mighty Name of the beloved Son You sent to redeem us all. Amen.

Ω

Hold on to an UN-"INVERTED" key to faithfulness:

But when the kindness and love of God our Savior appeared, he saved us, not because of righteous things we had done, but because of his mercy. He saved us through the washing of rebirth and renewal of the Holy Spirit, whom he poured out on us generously through Jesus Christ our Savior, so that having been justified by his grace, we might become heirs having the hope of eternal life.

Titus 3:4-7

IN 'S CONCLUSION

Completion of the Lord's High Priestly "IN" Prayer

IN **began with Jesus' prayer in John 17,** just before He went to the cross. As we come to the end of Revelation's scriptural foretaste that God has provided for us, we find Jesus' prayer fully answered. The Son is being united with His Bride; they are becoming "one," as the Son and the Father have been "one."

During His Incarnation, Jesus longed to share the fact of His oneness with the Father. His enemies wanted to kill Him for saying it (John 10:30-31), and it was hardly grasped, even by His closest friends. What did Jesus try so hard to get His disciples to see during His last night with them? When they asked to "see the Father," Jesus assured them that *"Anyone who has seen me has seen the Father.... Believe me when I say that I am in the Father and the Father is in me"* (John 14:9b, 11a). Jesus promised them that night that the Spirit would be soon moving from outside them to inside them, saying that *"he lives with you and will be in you"* (John 14:17b). He knew that His glorification was soon to happen, and with that, the outpouring of the Spirit would happen, too. He would actually take up residence within them! Their transformation after Pentecost proved the Spirit's indwelling Presence.

When we come to our Lord's High Priestly prayer just before He takes His own blood into the true Holy of Holies, we hear Him interceding with the Father, saying...

> *My prayer is not for them alone. I pray also for those who will believe in me through their message, that all of them may be one, Father, just as you are in me and I am in you. May they also be in us so that the world may believe*

that you have sent me...I have made you known to them, and will continue
to make you known in order that the love you have for me may be <u>in</u> *them,*
and that I myself may be <u>in</u> *them.*   ~ John 17:20-21, 26

One way to visualize the mystery of the relationships that Jesus is praying about is to envision a sphere representing the totality of being. Think of the outmost part of the sphere as representing the <u>Father</u>, *in* whom is Christ. The next layer inward is <u>Christ</u>, *in* whom is the believer. The next layer inward represents the <u>believer</u>, *in* whom dwells the Spirit. The core within the believer is the <u>Spirit of God</u>, Himself. *Can you envision those spheres within spheres?* The Messiah asked the Father that the kind of union the Father, Son, and Spirit enjoy be shared with the rest of the family. Amazing! God's goal goes beyond our salvation from the penalty of sin. His full redemption welcomes us into the very family of the Trinity!

What was Jesus' parting advice, made very simple? We can try to "put it all together" by intricate study, but Jesus knew our limitations, and often spoke very simply. He could not tell them all that was on His heart as He was about to depart, so in John 15:1-8, He gave His brothers and sisters one simple command that would cover everything for them. It would cover everything for any of the believers who would follow them historically, too. We know from John 17:20 that we later believers were on His heart as well! Jesus took a very common thing in Israel, a grapevine, and told them to see themselves as branches from His vine, through whom the Spirit of God flowed like sap. He is the Vine. "Abide in me" (KJV and RSV) — or "remain in me" (NIV), He said. He would do everything else. We don't produce the fruit, the sap does. We are just to stay connected. "Just" is simple, but it means earnestly choosing to stay in fellowship with Jesus. "Just" is sufficient, because <u>ALL</u> that He IS, is ours <u>IN</u> Christ.

Therefore, in this relay race called "life," may we faithfully pass on the torch that was passed to us!

Prayer: *Paul expressed the love that Jesus gave him for His body, the Church, in the following prayer. The Spirit can make it our prayer, as well.*

> I have become its servant by the commission God gave me to present to you the word of God in its fullness — the mystery that has been kept hidden for ages and generations, but is now disclosed to the saints. To them God has chosen to make known among the Gentiles the glorious riches of this mystery, which is Christ in you, the hope of glory. We proclaim him, admonishing and teaching everyone with all wisdom, so that we may present everyone perfect in Christ. To this end I labor, struggling with all his energy, which so powerfully works in me.

~ Colossians 1:25-29

Ω

My concluding thoughts about my experience of the Messiah as "ALL" and "IN"

♥ *How am I seeing and appreciating Jesus in a fuller way? A personal example:*

♥ *How am I seeing more of the panoramic unity of the Old and New Testaments? A specific example:*

♥ *How am I understanding more of God's overarching plan to redeem the world in relationship to the Jewish and Gentile communities? Some special insight:*

♥ *How am I experiencing a fuller grasp of some of the aspects of being "in Christ"? An example of one aspect:*

♥ *To which "therefore" (or "let us" or "so") response in Scripture am I more awake? (See pages 95-96, 111.) A specific response:*

♥ *How might I conserve and multiply what the Spirit has shown me? (Such as... to digest these studies in greater depth, memorize their key Scriptures, draw others into this kind of study, lead a study, or pass on the torch of faith in some other way.) My next step:*

My prayer:

The Kingdom View

The vantage point of the *IN* studies has been to search the Scriptures for God's message to us, and the goal has been for each of us to respond.

Oh that we could change the viewpoint — feel the warmth of the sun melting an ice-covered day, hear the swell of music, see the widening screen with deepening colors, bursting the bounds of language — that we might view the whole by looking down from the vantage point of God's exalted glory!

Creative musicians and writers have tried to awaken us to the marvels of God's redemptive narrative, using music and fiction as vehicles to rouse in us the kind of response that is commensurate with the magnificence of the fullness of the Kingdom of God.

Handel tried to do it in the Messiah Oratorio. C. S. Lewis's *Narnia* series pictured it in terms of Aslan's transformation of the children into kings and queens. Tolkien awakened our loyalty to Middle Earth's rightful heir, and thrilled us with *The Return of the King.*

Only the Holy Spirit can sing the song of Redemption in our hearts, melt our frozen-statue-like lethargy into a serving royal priesthood, and thrill us with the ecstasy of the return of the King of kings.

In our world, God has self-limited His Presence among us until He finishes His work of redemption. The Revelation of John begins to tear away the veil and disclose the reality of the Lamb become Lion, the fierce judgment of the Rider on the white horse, the exalted rule of the King of kings, the gentleness of the Prince of peace, and the tenderness of the Bridegroom's love. Words beg to express the dimension and size of His unrestrained Presence. Only the Spirit of God can lift us out of ourselves to stand in awe and in worship before the wonder of God — Father, Son, and Holy Spirit.

For Thine is the Kingdom,
and the power,
and the glory,
for ever and ever.
Amen!

Ω

APPENDIX

In Gem Visual
Key Verses

IN: John 17:20-26, Ephesians 1:3-14

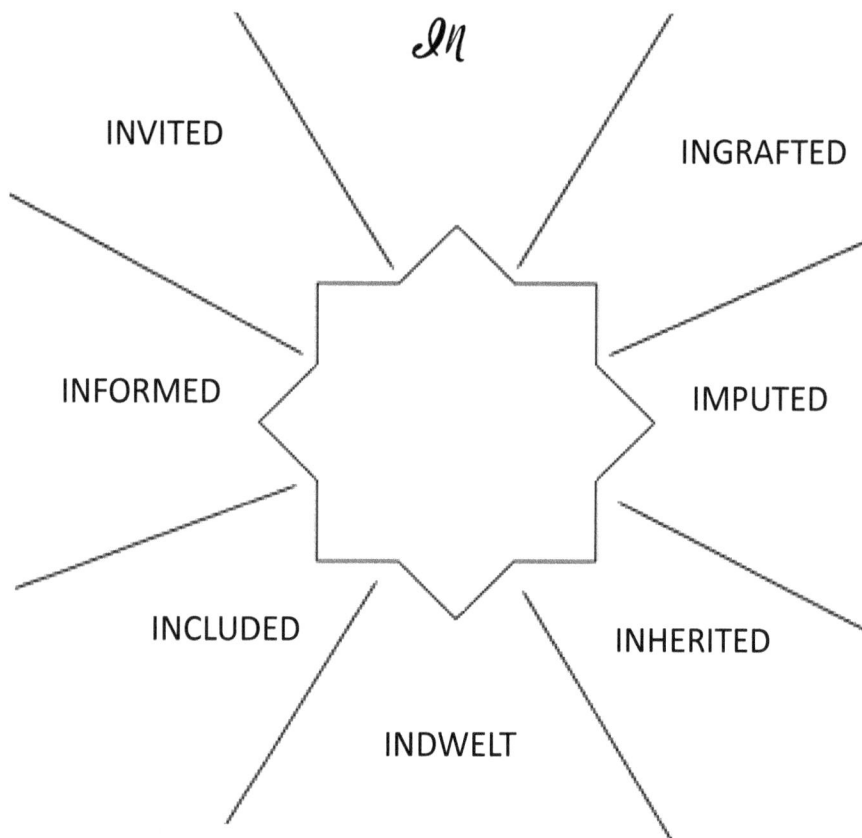

IN

INVITED

INGRAFTED

INFORMED

IMPUTED

INCLUDED

INHERITED

INDWELT

*ASPECTS OF THE MESSIAH'S
NEW COVENANT
INCARNATION IN HIS PEOPLE
THROUGH THE OUTPOURED SPIRIT*

(*Read the above illustration from 1:00 clockwise.*)
It depicts the riches given to all those in Christ. After the Son's
Incarnation in the Gospels and the Spirit's Inauguration in Acts, the
Letters and Revelation reveal precious "IN's" that are like facets of
the Bridegroom's engagement ring to His bride!

(*Match this visual with the accompanying Key Verses.*)

KEYS TO BEING *IN* CHRIST

INTEGRATION

In the past God spoke to our forefathers through the prophets at many times and in various ways, but in these last days he has spoken to us by his Son, whom he appointed heir of all things, and through whom he made the universe.

Hebrews 1:1-2

INCLUDED

And you also were included in Christ when you heard the word of truth, the gospel of your salvation. Having believed, you were marked in him with a seal, the promised Holy Spirit, who is a deposit guaranteeing our inheritance until the redemption of those who are God's possession - to the praise of his glory.

Ephesians 1:13-14

INCARNATION

In the beginning was the Word, and the Word was with God, and the Word was God. He was with God in the beginning. ...The Word became flesh, and made his dwelling among us. We have seen his glory, the glory of the One and Only, who came from the Father, full of grace and truth.

John 1:1-2, 14

INDWELT

To them God has chosen to make known among the Gentiles the glorious riches of this mystery, which is Christ in you, the hope of glory.

Colossians 1:27

INAUGURATION

Exalted to the right hand of God, He has received from the Father the promised Holy Spirit and has poured out what you now see and hear.

Acts 2:33

INHERITED

For this reason Christ is the mediator of a new covenant, that those who are called may receive the promised eternal inheritance - now that he has died as a ransom to set them free from the sins committed under the first covenant.

Hebrews 9:15

INGRAFTED

If some of the branches have been broken off, and you, though a wild olive shoot, have been grafted in among the others and now share in the nourishing sap from the olive root, do not boast over those branches. If you do, consider this: You do not support the root, but the root supports you.

Romans 11:17-18

INFORMED

"Do not be afraid. I am the First and the Last. I am the Living One; I was dead, and behold I am alive for ever and ever! And I hold the keys of death and Hades. Write, therefore, what you have seen, what is now and what will take place later."

Revelation 1:17b-19

IMPUTED

Consider Abraham: "He believed God, and it was credited to him as righteousness." Understand, then, that those who believe are children of Abraham. The Scripture foresaw that God would justify the Gentiles by faith, and announced the gospel in advance to Abraham. "All nations will be blessed through you." So those who have faith are blessed along with Abraham, the man of faith.

Galatians 3:6-9

INVITED

Then the angel said to me, "Write: blessed are those who are invited to the wedding supper of the Lamb!" And he added, "These are the true words of God."

Revelation 19:9

BIBLIOGRAPHY and RESOURCES

Bernis, Jonathan, "Roadblocks to Redemption" *Jewish Voice Today Magazine, September/October 2008.*

Bruce, F. F., *Are the New Testament Documents Reliable?* First edition, published in England in 1943. Sixth edition: *The New Testament Documents: Are they reliable?* William B. Eerdmans Publishing Company, Grand Rapids, Michigan, l981.

Bunyan, *Pilgrim's Progress,* originally published in England in 1678. There are many versions today. One with the original illustrations is published by Suzeteo Enterprises, Greenwood, Wisconsin, 2011.

Fox's Book of Martyrs, edited by Wm. Byron Forbush, Universal Book and Bible House, Philadelphia, Pennsylvania. Copyright, l926 by The John C. Winston Company.

Jones, E. Stanley, *The Word Became Flesh,* Abingdon, Nashville, l963.

Lewis, C.S., The *Narnia* Series, Book seven: *The Last Battle*, Collier Books, New York, New York, second printing l971.

Nee, Watchman, *The Normal Christian Life,* Christian Literature Crusade, Fort Washington, Pennsylvania, paperback edition reprinted l965.

Sanders, J. Oswald, *Christ Indwelling and Enthroned,* Marshall, Morgan, and Scott, Edinburg; Van Kampen Press, Wheaton, Illinois, USA, l949.

Tolkien, J. R. R., *The Lord of the Rings* Part III, *The Return of the King*, Ballantine Books, New York, New York, 1994.

Verduin, Leonard, *The Reformers and Their Stepchildren*, Eerdmans, l964. Reprinted by The Christian Hymnary Publishers, Grand Rapids, Michigan, 2004.

Helpful background resources for leading ALL, IN and Therefore studies:

THE MESSIAH MYSTERY
The Old and New Testaments' Inseparable Disclosure
by Charles and Kay Bascom.
Revised 2006, LSI, 325 pages
(24 Power Point lessons on CD also available from the authors)

KEYS TO THE MESSIAH MYSTERY
Teaching resources to accompany the larger text
by Kay Bascom.
2006, LSI, 100 pages
*(Both orderable through local Christian bookstores,
or on-line from BarnesandNoble.com or Amazon.com)*

Companion twelve-chapter interactive Bible studies by Kay Bascom:

ALL
**Tracing the Messiah throughout
the Old Testament to the New,**
revealed by His prefigured and fulfilled roles.
2017, 136 pages, 5.5 x 8.5

Therefore
**Who *Yeshua* said He is, how He fulfilled the Old Covenant,
who He is in His culture, who the apostles said He is,**
and what our response should *Therefore* be.
2017, 160 pages, 5.5 x 8.5
*(Both may be ordered at OlivePressPublisher.com, local bookstores,
or on-line from BarnesandNoble.com or Amazon.com, etc.)*